Little BIG Conversations

*Get your kids talking and thinking
in fast and fun ways*

K A V I N   W A D H A R

*Dad of two kids
Founder of KidCoach*

DEDICATION

To my mum: the best coach of kids I know

Table of Contents

Foreword by Ian Gilbert (Thunks)

"My brain hurts."

This is a book about thinking. It is also a book about talking. Both are important for children. Indeed, a paediatric neurologist associate of mine once assured me that, when it comes to young children, talking and thinking are the same thing anyway.

I have been having conversations with children and young people designed to get their brains to hurt for many years.

The thing that fired me up about what is unleashed when you really allow children to think was a thinking skills programme that grew out of the US a few decades ago. Philosophy for Children – also known as 'P4C' if you fancy a quick Google – is one of the few thinking programmes academically proven to be of benefit to youngsters. This programme understands we are born philosophers but this desire to be curious, to look deeply and to question gets sort of lost along the way as we start to play the game of school. Here, unless we are very lucky, the system means remembering will trump creativity and knowledge will be prioritised over thinking our own thoughts.

Out of my work in schools with P4C evolved what came to be known (and for the life of me I cannot remember the exact point this happened) as Thunks.[1]

A Thunk is a deceptively fiendish question that makes you think because, with a Thunk, there are no correct answers and thinking is all you've got. These are all Thunks:

- *Is a broken-down car parked?*
- *Is it OK to bully a bully?*
- *Is there more future than past?*
- *Is a pregnant woman two people?*

The fact that so many successful schools globally seem to love using my Thunks testifies to the fact that you can get children thinking and doing well in school. In this way, you can build confidence, self-esteem, oracy, teamwork, critical thought, philosophical questioning, curiosity and develop a love of thinking, without taking your eye off the 'do well at school' goals many parents have for their children.

That's the thing with us parents. Of course, we want the best for our children. But it's bigger than that, isn't it? Being successful also means we don't prioritise academic success over well-being, that we help them develop these all-important social skills, that we help them become rounded, ethical adults and we help them become creative, critical thinkers in the process.

That's why when I met Kavin in 2019 I was immediately struck with what he was trying to do - fast and fun chats to help parents get their kids talking and thinking. He had come across my Thunks work and 'reached out' as they say these days.

Before I knew it, I was part of the KidCoach journey, offering moral support to Kavin as he wrote better and better questions to put into his app for parents to use with their children.

Kavin's work is, rightly, focussed on developing 21ˢᵗ century skills in children. For example, the current World Economic Forum list of 'trending skills' for 2025 mentions the need for 'analytical thinking and innovation' in its number one spot.[2] Understanding things isn't enough; it's what you create that's new that counts (the Latin word for new, 'novus', is at the heart of words like 'innovation' and 'novel'). What's more, number five on the World Economic Forum's list is 'creativity, originality and initiative' while, new at number ten, you'll find 'ideation' next to 'reasoning' and 'problem-solving'.

These skills will take you much further than simply knowing stuff. Everyone knows stuff. Knowledge isn't power, it's what you do with it that matters.

That's why I love the KidCoach approach to getting children talking and thinking. It helps parents to channel their children's natural ability to look around and ask *Why?* Or sometimes better *Why not?* It gives them the message that thinking for themselves is not only important, it's also great fun. It says to a child, your opinion matters. It reassures them their perspective on the world matters too. And it also is a process through which parents talk 'with' – not 'at' or 'down to' or 'across' – their children. Which is a wonderful thing in and of itself in this busy world we live in.

Enjoy the many strategies in this book - and the app if you give it a go – and have fun spending time with your child or children as you do. There's a handy list of questions to refer to in the Appendix and I know you will want to take a close look at Chapter Five, which shows you how to take any conversation and go a whole lot deeper in true P4C style.

And if at the end of it all, you hear your kids saying "my brain hurts", take heart in knowing you have done a great job.

Ian Gilbert
Author of Thunks
Founder – Independent Thinking[3]
July 2022

Introduction: It's such a simple idea

"A well-worded question is the quickest way to connect after a long day."

Dr Anne Fishel - Founder of
The Family Dinner Project

Author's note

When did you last ask your kids a question they weren't expecting?

A few years ago I started getting 'deja vu' every time I had a chat with my kids. Being the busy working parents we are, my wife and I always seemed to have the same hurried and objective-driven conversations with our two children.

- *How was school today?*
- *Have you done your homework?*
- *Can you pick that up?*
- *Have you tidied your toys?*
- *Are you ready to go?*

You might experience something similar in your home and if so you should know you are not alone. One study showed that 80% of the language adults use with children are 'commands.'[1]

At the same time I was working in a large multinational company. It struck me that the graduates we recruited all had glowing CVs / resumes, but couldn't think for themselves or communicate very well with others. You may have experienced something similar.

So I started thinking we could get a 'two for one'.

What if parents at home were inspired to have fun and new conversations with their kids, which gave them lots of practice at talking on the spot and thinking for themselves?

What if this could transform 'transactional talk' in homes into 'coaching moments' for kids to build the key skills they need to thrive in the modern world?

What if this could all be done in a way that was fast, fun and didn't feel like learning so kids would engage and families would end up building some lovely memories of conversations they had?

Thus was born the concept of KidCoach.

This was the banner under which I started writing lots of fast, fun and thought-provoking questions for kids which build key skills.

I was so passionate about this idea that I quit my corporate job to pursue it. I honestly believed, and still do today, that our kids will need a new set of 21st century skills to thrive and we as parents are extremely well placed to help them develop these skills.

These were some of the first few conversation starters I wrote:

- *What are 10 things to do with a cup?* (Creativity)
- *Is there life on other planets?* (Critical Thinking)
- *When is it good to fail at something?* (Resilience)
- *How would you describe a car to an alien?* (Communication)
- *Who is a leader you admire and why?* (Leadership)

I shared them with other parents who enjoyed the conversations they sparked and asked me for lots more. I was happy to do this but also conscious there were lots of experts out there who could probably guide me better.

My research led very quickly to 'Philosophy for Children' and 'Oracy', which are movements in some schools to get kids talking and thinking more in class. I reached out to their key leaders and also other experts, from child psychologists to parenting coaches, who helped me to think about how to make these questions effective for the home environment.

Now better equipped, I worked closely with our early-adopter parents who were trying out this new content and giving me constant feedback. It turns out they wanted all these questions and prompts in a handy app, so I turned to a tech-savvy friend of mine to build a working prototype.

We called it the 'KidCoachApp' and it launched in 2020. Since then it has been constantly iterated and improved upon and I am so pleased to say at the time of writing it has been downloaded thousands of times and holds a 5.0 star rating in both the Apple and Google app stores.

Around the same time I also started a podcast called 'Questions To Ask Your Kids.' This is a show where I ask 6-12 year old children some questions from the app, simulating the kind of discussion I am trying to inspire in homes around the world. Each episode is a short 10-15 minutes and my hope is it illustrates ways in which we could all have these sorts of conversations. I've had 100+ chats with different kids so far and loved every moment of it. It's always amazing what kids come up with and it's also been helpful to go back and make the original question better as we learn what works or not in practice.

All of this is to say that I've been working super hard since 2019, learning how to have great conversations with children and writing thousands of questions to help families like yours.

As I've been sharing what I've learned I found myself writing 50+ articles, appearing on 20+ podcast shows and even featured in 10+ newspapers. Each time I found myself sharing different snippets and after a while I felt I should write them all down in a simple and structured way.

That's what this book is.

If you are reading this then you have decided to invest your time in my book, for which I thank you. I know you are busy so I appreciate it enormously.

I've kept the book fast and fun. It is about 10 chapters long and each will take you about 10 minutes to read. It is shorter than most parenting books and that is very deliberate. I just wanted to get the key messages across to you with as little fluff as possible.

There are three parts.

Part A asks why you need to do this. I explain why the world is changing so fast and why conversations are such a great way to build the skills your kids will need to thrive in it.

Part B helps you with what to ask your kids. I'll give you a ton of question examples, follow-on prompts and share real life examples of dialogues with different children.

Part C tackles the how of it. As parents we often want to do new things but don't know how to get started or how to overcome obstacles in our routine, so I'll give you some practical ideas and tips to get past this.

I've also pulled together a super handy Appendix section for you. Here you will find nearly 100 question examples you can refer to wherever you want.

So keep this book handy on a coffee table somewhere.

A final note on the name.

At first I didn't know what to call the book so I shared a few possible titles on social media and asked my parent community which they preferred. The runaway winner was 'Little Big Conversations'.

I was secretly pleased since I think this title embodies many important dimensions we will explore together. That we are Big people having conversations with Little people; that we are building Big important skills but in Little and fun ways; and that our chats will create Big memories for life that just take Little moments to create.

Happy reading, and whatever happens next, I hope you have a wonderful conversation with your kids tonight.

Yours,

Kavin Wadhar
Dad of two kids
www.kidcoach.app

Terminology

This is a book for parents of children. But of course there are many grown-ups who have a vested interest in the development of a young child. Guardians, caregivers, uncles and aunts, grandparents, older siblings and many others. Since it would be quite a mouthful to mention these every time please forgive me for abbreviating all of the above to 'parents' for the rest of this book.

I also refer a few times to 'schools' referencing them as the educational institution many children go to. This is a simplification as I know there are many types of educational options out there, with an increasing number of families 'homeschooling' or 'home educating' for example. Again, please forgive me for this simplification.

PART A: WHY?

CHAPTER 1

Why will my child need a different set of skills to thrive in tomorrow's world?

"In real life, I assure you, there is no such thing as algebra."

Fran Lebowitz - Author, Speaker and Actor

We have absolutely no idea what our children will do when they grow up. None. Zilch. Nada.

Gone are the days when we could train someone up for a job for life. The world is just changing too quickly.

As medicine improves, a 10-year-old today could live to over 100 and perhaps work for over 70 years of that. Meanwhile, the world will change several times over.

How can you train a child up in the first 20 years of their life, for the next 70+ ever-changing years?

You can't. It's impossible.

Consider that just 20 years ago smartphones were not widespread. Facebook had not been invented yet and Google had only just been launched. Who knows what will happen in the next 20 years? And the 20 years after that?

Jobs are changing quickly

The Institute for the Future said in 2017 that "85% of the jobs that will exist in 2030 have not even been invented yet."[1]

You can easily see this being true. Just look at these jobs that are fairly common today - how many of these existed 20 years ago?

- Professional blogger
- Big data analyst
- Social media influencer

The pace of change is mind-blowing and it's only increasing. All sorts of new technologies are on the rise and promise to change our world in the blink of an eye, such as:

- Driverless cars so we can work while we commute
- 3D printing so we can manufacture anything we want at home ourselves
- Bioengineering so new limbs and organs can keep us living for longer

Much of this tech will be powered by Artificial Intelligence (AI). This term gets a lot of attention nowadays. The simple definition of AI is "the ability of a computer or computer-controlled robot to perform tasks commonly associated with intelligent beings" (Britannica).[2]

Right now the tasks AI is doing tend to be labour-intensive and repetitive tasks such as:

- Switchboard operators
- Bridge toll collectors
- Train ticket dispensers

As AI continues improving it is feasible some other jobs will start to be replaced, e.g.

- Receptionists
- Couriers
- Taxi drivers

But in their place different types of jobs will spring up we humans are beautifully suited to.

Consider these examples from a Cognizant whitepaper:[3]

- Bring-your-own-IT-facilitator – helping employees connect all their personal technology to the company they have started working at.
- Ethical sourcing officer – ensuring companies are buying sustainably and not just based on algorithmic recommendations.
- Walker/Talker for the elderly – spending time with people who are living longer and longer to give them the emotional and social support they need.

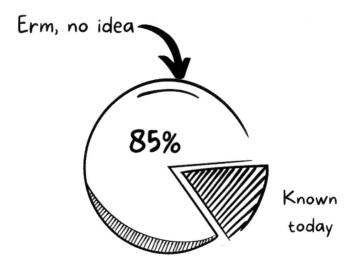

Fig 1: Jobs Our Kids Will Have

New skills are needed

What do each of these new jobs have in common?

They all require a high degree of 'human' or '21st-century' skills.

- A Bring-Your-Own-IT Facilitator will need to communicate well with lots of different people, understand their needs and help them find a solution.
- An Ethical sourcing officer will need to make philosophical choices about the best way to reduce harm through their company's actions.
- A Walker/Talker for the Elderly will need to have lots of empathy and social skills as they chat with their client and help them enjoy their life.

As the Organisation for Economic Cooperation and Development (OECD) said "The future is about pairing the artificial intelligence of computers with the cognitive, social and emotional skills and values of humans. It's going to be our imagination, our awareness and our sense of responsibility that will allow us to harness technology to shape our world for the better."[4]

I think it's great that in many cases we will be able to outsource the heavy-lifting work to the machines, so we can focus on using our creativity, empathy and other human skills.

So which skills will my kids need?

There is a lot of research on this and as you might expect they don't all say the same thing. Thankfully there are areas of overlap and agreement.

Here are three skills frameworks I think are worth mentioning, and below I will summarise for you my key takeaways.

1. McKinsey, the management consultants, put together a report in 2018[5] highlighting the shift in workplace skills needed for the future. In their 'higher cognitive' and 'social and emotional' categories they highlight the following soft skills – critical thinking, project management, information processing, creativity, communication, negotiation, leadership, entrepreneurship, adaptability, teaching.[6]

2. Pearson, the international education company, has a collection of resources to help get students work-ready, summarised by this statement: "Based on an

extensive review of existing 21st-century frameworks, academic research, and labour market trends, Pearson has identified six common skill sets that are crucial for employability: critical and creative thinking, communication, collaboration and teamwork, self-management, social responsibility, and leadership."[7]

3. Skills Builder, a UK-based partnership working with over 10,000 teachers and 700 organisations, has built an umbrella framework of eight essential skills they are championing: speaking, listening, creativity, problem solving, staying positive, aiming high, teamwork and leadership.[8]

Two key takeaways

OK, that was a lot of information. Here are two key takeaways.

First is the specific skills of creativity, communication and critical thinking seem to be the top three that feature in all frameworks. These also seem to be the most commonly sought-after skills among the thousands of parents I have worked with.

Second is there are three broad groups of skills: social, cognitive and emotional. Each of these will have a few other skills embedded within. This is an easier way of remembering to keep our children's skill set broad and balanced. Social skills would include things like communication and leadership; cognitive skills would encompass thinking critically and analytically; emotional skills would include working on being empathetic, present and the ability to regulate your own emotions.

In layperson's terms, I call this 'talking, thinking and feeling' and this is the structure I used to build my app. See Appendix I for more details on this and the 12 skills I focus on.

If all of this is getting too technical then don't worry. As parents, I don't think it matters which framework we work towards. We just need to make sure we are preparing our kids for the world of tomorrow by encouraging a range of skills to be developed.

These skills are already in demand

Employers have long been calling for graduates entering the workforce to have a more well-rounded skill set.

As the LinkedIn CEO Jeff Weiner said in 2018: "The biggest gap employers see is in interpersonal skills."

Who better to summarise what employers need than the head of the de facto social platform for all job hunters, HR professionals and recruitment agents?

In an interview with WIRED magazine, Jeff Weiner said the majority of people think coding and software skills are the most in demand, but goes on to say that actually what matters more is the impact technology has on society and how we humans are going to adapt to this.

That's the bit we are all missing.

The LinkedIn boss continued:[9]

"The biggest skills gap...is soft skills. Written communication, oral communication, team building, people leadership, collaboration. For jobs like sales, sales development, business development, customer service..."

This demand for soft skills is universal. To cite another report, the Sutton Trust in 2017 found "94% of employers agree that [soft] skills are as or more important than academic qualifications."[10]

It's not to say maths, English, science or any other key subjects aren't important. It's just that as a society we need to massively increase the focus on softer skills that have traditionally had a smaller focus in our children's learning programmes.

Expert Insights:
Tom Ravenscroft - Founder & CEO of the Skills Builder Partnership [8]

I started my career as a secondary school teacher in London back in 2007. It became very clear to me very quickly there was a huge gap in the curriculum. While every moment was focused on trying to boost grades, there was no similar focus on the other bits of education that surely matter just as much as knowledge: building essential skills like communication, creativity, self-management and collaboration.

Thorough research has shown these essential skills are linked with increased career aspirations and earnings, wellbeing, and educational attainment. They also boost children's ability to persevere and improve their sense of self-efficacy – that is, their sense that they are in control of their own destiny. Surely we want that for every child?

In 2009, I set up the Skills Builder Partnership to look at how we could work together to transform the education system so every child and young person got the opportunity to build these critical skills as part of their education. We've made good progress, and more than 1.4 million learners developed their essential skills using the Skills Builder approach in the last year.

Critically though, we learned that while what happens in the classroom is important, it is not enough. The Partnership now includes fantastic organisations like KidCoach because the importance of parents and carers in boosting their children's essential skills is paramount.

Our latest piece of research shows parental engagement with their children's education makes a huge difference. Learners in the bottom quartile for essential skill development had parents who were 22% less likely to be involved in their child's education.

Most compellingly to me though, I have the experience of being a parent of two boys of four and seven years old. The conversational approach outlined in this book is exactly the sort of deliberate reflection and practice that makes all the difference in building children's essential skills. They are fantastic ways for parents to support what matters and they're a lot of fun too.

You know this makes sense already

The need for more 21st century skill development in our children is intuitive.

Just consider your own workplace.

Be it a hospital, bank, accounting firm, school or supermarket – the most successful employees are the ones who present themselves well, communicate in a compelling way, think fast on their feet, are empathetic to those around them and work well in teams. Right?

We all know the phrase 'It's not what you know, but who you know.' I dislike it, since it suggests schmoozing is the way to success, but there is an element of truth in it – the way we interact with people matters an awful lot.

So what can be done?

It's worth saying that schools, teachers and education experts acknowledge all of the above. They completely understand the importance of both academics and 21st-century skills.

Just take the late, great educationalist - Sir Ken Robinson. A fantastic champion for what he called the 8Cs – creativity, critical thinking, communication, compassion, collaboration etc. His TED talk from 2006 about 'Do Schools Kill Creativity?' remains the most viewed ever with 70m+ views[11]. Throughout the talk he speaks about how "creativity is as important as literacy" and makes the case for much more focus needed on his 8Cs.

The OECD Director of Education and Skills also put it extremely well in 2020: "Schools need to develop first-class humans, not second-class robots".[12] What did he mean? Simply that if we only trained children in academic areas like maths and English, then they are destined to be these second-class robots. Why? Computers will always be able to crunch numbers and process text far better than humans ever can. We can't out-robot a robot. So let's not even try. However, it is where quintessential human skills are involved like creativity, empathy and leadership where robots will have a hard time keeping up with us. So let's get first-class at these human qualities.

The Sutton Trust explains how the balance between 'robot' academic and 'human' 21st-century skills needs improving. In their Life Lessons Report in 2017, they said, "While young people are painfully aware of the importance of getting good grades and under incredible pressure to achieve them, this report shows that the life and character skills considered key to success in their working lives are at risk of being overlooked."[13]

A survey in the Sutton Trust report polled teachers and found "97% of teachers agree that [soft] skills are as or more important than academic qualifications."[15]

Even with that consensus however, the Prince's Trust report in the same year found "91% of teachers think schools should be doing more to help students develop soft skills."[14]

So something is wrong.

People working in the education system are almost unanimous in their opinion that soft or 21st-century skills are incredibly important to develop and yet also say that not enough is being done and we need to focus more on them.

I know this is a well-documented problem and I also know there are many smart, dedicated education experts (far more expert than me) looking into it. But while mainstream school systems continue to have high amounts of regulation, with a focus on exam-passing rather than skill-building, I'm not sure things will change that quickly.

Don't worry though.

As a parent, there are simple things you can do at home independently of 'the system' to help your kids build a variety of the 21st-century skills they need.

CHAPTER 2

Why am I so well placed to do something about this as a parent?

"At the end of the day the most overwhelming key to a child's success is the positive involvement of their parents."

Jane D Hull - American Politician and Educator

Parents.

Is there a more evocative word?

For each of us it can give rise to many thoughts, feelings, images and memories. Not only for a child but even as an adult who thinks back to their childhood, the people who raise us are a massive part of all of us.

For the average child nowadays there is no greater developmental force than parents (or their primary caregiver).

The Power of Parents

Here is a question most people get wrong.

What proportion of their time could a child spend at school? Take their waking hours only and consider it across the year.

Is it 80%, 50% or 20% at school?

20% sounds way too low so it can't be that.

Or can it?

Let's do the maths:

- 24 hours a day x 365 days a year = 9,000 hours a year.
- Of these, about 1/3 spent sleeping so let's say 6,000 hours awake.
- How many of these hours could then be spent at school?
- Say 35 school weeks a year x 5 days a week x 7 hours a day = 1,200 hours at school.
- 1,200 hours at school/6,000 waking hours in the year = a mere 20% of a child's waking hours could be spent at school.

Put another way, at least a whopping 80% of your kids' waking hours would be spent at home. With you or another caregiver.

Does that surprise you?

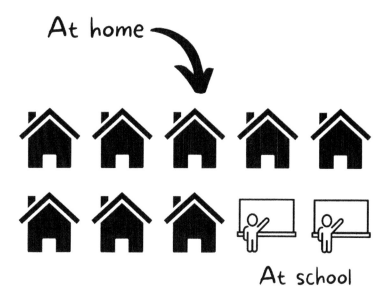

Fig 2: How School Children Spend Their Time

Busy, busy, busy

As a parent myself however, I know this time flies by. Life is super hectic nowadays and it never feels like we have a moment to spare. Commuting to work, preparing dinner, doing the school run, ferrying around the kids to extracurricular activities (including at the weekend), paying the bills, doing bathtimes and bedtimes, before finally squeezing in 30 minutes of Netflix at the end of the day to unwind.

If your children are in school, some of the time carved out to converse with them may be to help with their homework. While I do not recommend skipping homework, the words of Michael Parker (M.Ed), author of Talk With Your Kids, comes to mind: "Millions of parents are out there at the moment drilling their children with extra comprehension grammar and maths questions ...I doubt that these are producing engaged, quality discussions between parents and children."[1]

One thing I have noticed though is we do all get odd pockets of time here and there with the kids. You might know what I mean, maybe it is during your short drive home or while chopping the vegetables for dinner or when putting them to bed. So maybe we can use this time to help shape and develop them in a way traditional schools can't?

Each moment is vanishingly short, but does exist, if you are ready to capture it.

Capturing the moment

I read a bedtime story to my daughter, Mia, every evening. One time we were reading an Aesop's Fable – the one called The Wind and the Sun. You might know it, it's one of my favourite fables.

A man is walking along and he has a coat on. The Wind and the Sun have a bet, to see who can get the man to take his coat off first. The Wind goes up first and uses force. He blows and blows really hard, but of course the man just gets colder and pulls his coat tighter around him. Then the Sun has a go. He shines warmly and since the man gets hot, he wants to take the coat off himself. So the Sun wins the bet, because the moral of the story is you can't force anybody to do anything, it has to come from within.

Obvious, right?

Well, it wasn't so obvious to my young daughter, because she immediately asked me, "But why daddy? The wind is really strong. Can't he just blow the coat off the man?" And this led very naturally into a discussion around leadership and persuasion, and how we need to use kindness and not force to motivate people.

Now this discussion only lasted five minutes or so, but I knew right there and then that this was an idea she would remember for life. This little 'coaching moment', done simply through conversation, took just five minutes and required no preparation or materials.

She went soundly to sleep afterwards and I went to bed also with a high-five parenting feeling of a job well done.

You are your child's perfect coach

If your children are in school, right now you might be thinking – surely this sort of development is the school's job? I don't have the time, interest and / or capability to do what a teacher can do in the classroom.

Well, it's true we don't all have teacher training, but consider what we do have:

- We are adults with rich life experiences to share.
- We know our children much better than a teacher does.
- We spend more time with them than anyone else.

Ask any teacher – they would jump at the chance to:

- Have a class size of just one or two kids.
- Be an expert in what makes their students tick.
- Need zero preparation or materials.

Yet that is exactly the situation we can embrace each and every day – during one of these 'coaching moments' we are presented with.

Parent Stories:
Suzy - mum of eight and 10 year old

It falls to us parents to nurture an environment of questioning and exploration. When something as simple as a conversation can help us parents take part in their education like this then why would you not give it a go?

With my autistic son, we are working on perspective-taking. It's helpful for him to realise other people might have different views to him and to become comfortable with this. All the questions I ask are open-ended with lots of possible ways someone might think about them, so this helps him think of those other opinions.

Once we were covering World War Two and my son had lots of questions about this at the time. So I asked *Are wars between countries ever a good thing?* This got us talking about how sometimes war has to happen to protect others but also it normally ends up worsening the situation. My eldest son then went on to say he wants to work in government and make sure we never go to war.

A natural approach

What I am describing is nothing new.

Humans have been educating their young for thousands of years through the 'village community' – the notion there is an ecosystem of adults around children who tell them stories, model tasks, ask them questions and generally talk with them to impart skills – starting with parents.

The institution of schools is actually a fairly recent 'invention' which only went mainstream in the 1800s. While it had a specific purpose that has worked for some families, the point is there were other modalities in existence beforehand to educate kids and which are still present today.

A gold standard example

What can we learn from Esther Wojcicki? She raised 2 daughters – one became the CEO of YouTube and the other the co-founder and CEO of 23andme – so she is now something of a "famous" parent.

In interviews, she talks a lot about developing 21st-century skills through parenting. There is no mention of mainstream schooling.

She illustrates these three examples of building skills.

- Kindness: by involving themselves in the community, showing they cared about the people around them, asking their children what they can be doing to help others.

- Grit: by creating a safe space to let their children try new things, talking about how failure is OK as long as you learn from it, and coaching them to bounce right back and try again.
- Creativity: by looking for problems to solve, never being satisfied by the status quo, always asking how something could be done better.

As Esther says: "I've met lots of unhappy millionaires and even some unhappy billionaires. A lot of them probably started out as directionless kids....[but] everywhere there's a problem to be solved, someone or some group to support and champion. It really is a way of being in the world, and when it comes to our kids, it pays to shape this perspective as early as possible."[2]

Expert Insights:
Nicola Crompton - Specialist Teacher and Trainer for 20+ years and founder of Happy Home Learning UK[3]

We've all been there. The homework, dinner, bath, story, and bedtime routine can feel relentless. Our attention is yanked in a thousand directions and finding the time to support our child's learning can often be a challenge. So on days when we feel frazzled, the humble conversation starter can help us to reconnect with our children and offers helpful opportunities to learn stealthily together.

I am often asked how to help children become more confident. I believe the questioning approach also provides the perfect vehicle for boosting our children's confidence and for strengthening our relationship with them. I am a big advocate of using these 'open' questions in the classroom too: *If you could be anyone from a book, who would you be and why?*

Unlike so many worksheets, questions like these have no right or wrong answers. Instead, they offer your child the freedom to be creative and provide opportunities for your child to listen attentively to others and to respectfully agree and disagree with their views.

Parents are uniquely placed to support turn-taking skills and to help children form original views. It just requires practice. Initially, my 5-year-old daughter Edith would agree with her big sister and simply repeat what she had just said. You can imagine my delight when she recently acquired the ability to respectfully disagree: "No I don't think it would be a good idea to live forever, because..."

Conversations like these support learning away from the traditional methods of sitting at the table with paper and pen. You can pepper questions in on a walk, when eating out or even during bath times. I recommend writing down a small number of 'open' questions on a topic that interests your child. Invite your child to choose which question they would like everyone to answer. Children thrive on being provided with choices, however small they may seem.

You can do this too

Here is a super simple exercise to get you in the groove of finding these coaching moments.

Next time you are walking down the high street with your child, try the following:

- Give directions: *How do you get from home to the supermarket?* (Communication)
- Notice your surroundings: *What makes each house different?* (Critical Thinking)
- Spot a person on your walk: *How do you think they are feeling and why?* (Empathy)
- Talk about the shops: *If you could open your own shop, what would it sell and what would you call it?* (Creativity)

It has brought me so much joy to hear stories from the parents we work with at KidCoach. Many tell me how they have been inspired to have more 'coaching conversations' with their children. How these conversations have scratched beneath the surface and helped them bond with their children while, at the same time, preparing them for the world of tomorrow.

One mum told me recently we have inspired her to do a regular 'walk and talk' with her 8-year-old daughter, who as a result has gone from a closed book to an open chatterbox.

Similarly, a dad of a 7-year-old found the questions inspired him to start looking for the 'coaching moment' in everyday occurrences like walking down the street, and he is now coming up with all sorts of interesting questions himself.

You'll notice this method of coaching kids holds conversations at the centre. And you might be wondering why that takes precedence compared with reading a book together or doing some sort of activity. The next chapter reveals why the humble conversation is one of the most powerful parenting tools you have in your locker.

CHAPTER 3

Why is the humble conversation such a powerful tool?

"The way we talk to our children becomes their inner voice."

Peggy O'Mara - Former Editor of Mothering Magazine

It's 6pm in the evening. You've had a busy stressful day at work. The kitchen sink is piled high with dishes, dinner still needs preparation and the kids still need to do their homework.

You're feeling tired and increasingly exasperated. Maybe you're having one of those moments where you are wondering if you are being a good parent or "doing" parenting well.

If you ever feel like this, you are not alone. This is how I've felt half the time for sure. I think most of us feel this way with the busy, hectic modern lives we lead. Having to juggle work, the house, the kids - not to mention ourselves and our relationships with family, friends and partners.

But there is some good news.

As occupied as our legs might be running around after the kids, or our hands might be preparing dinner, we always have our voices free. We always have the ability to talk, ask questions and get into a good conversation.

Even if just for 5-10 minutes, we can all have a quick chat with our kids.

Conversations can be done anywhere, anytime

I'm so lucky to be able to talk with thousands of parents through the work I do. Each of these parents have got into a groove of having more and better conversations with their children. They do this in lots of different places, but the top five always seem to be:

1. In the car
2. On the school run
3. Lying in bed
4. Waiting for something
5. At the dinner table

Look at this list. Is there anything else you can do with your kids in all of these places?

That's why I am such an enthusiastic endorser of the humble conversation.

There are other wholesome ways to spend time with our kids, of course. Reading books, playing board games, cooking together etc. All of these have their time and place but, for me, nothing quite rivals the power and effect of a good conversation. Unlike books, they can be very current, such as talking about the news. Unlike board games, they are quick to start, needing no preparation. Unlike cooking dinner, they will not make a mess.

Not to say you shouldn't do these other things as well of course - reading, in particular, has tremendous benefits and widens our children's horizons, cooking together teaches a multitude of keylife skills and board games are an amazing way of spending quality time.

However, conversations are certainly better than just watching TV or putting our kids in front of YouTube.

Don't get me wrong, there are evenings when I do need to outsource parenting to the iPad, but equally I am always conscious of wanting to launch more meaningful and memorable conversations with my kids.

Fig 3: All The Places Conversations Work

Parent Stories:
Sonal - mum of five and eight year old

I live in the UK and work in Corporate Tax. I've been asking my kids quirky questions for several months now and I must say I really love the approach.

For example, we talked about *If we got a new pet, how would we look after it?* My younger son has asked for a cat, and this question really got him thinking about all the things he would need to do to care for the cat.

Car journeys, meal times, or even sofa times are more interesting and meaningful now as I'm developing my kids' minds in all sorts of ways.

I feel like over just a few months, their approach to being asked random questions has developed from an "I don't know" to actually pausing and thinking about a response.

Conversations build memories

Numerous studies show humans remember emotions more than they remember facts. Conversations with our kids about life events - overcoming issues with friends, practising hard to get on the football team, coming first in a maths competition - will reinforce these and help you both remember them for a lifetime.

I know it's fun to make grand gestures as a parent. Buying an expensive toy, throwing a lavish birthday party or going on an amazing beach holiday are just a few examples. However, I would argue it's the small things, repeatedly done, that truly matter to kids. Little habits and traditions seem to etch themselves deeper into their memories far more than one-off extravaganzas.

So if you have little conversational moments at the breakfast table most mornings then that is something your children will likely remember and cherish. More so than even that awesome Disneyland trip to see Mickey Mouse perhaps?

Something I remember

I must have been about 8 years old. We had a family day out in London. A big, scary and alien place to little old me. I remember we were on our way to lunch at McDonald's when we passed a homeless man in the street.

I'd seen these sorts of things on TV or read about them in books, but this was probably the first time I had seen something like this in person. I slowed down as we walked past to read his cardboard sign: "I'm hungry." I felt something strange in my own stomach but, like everyone else seemed to be doing, I continued walking past the man and to our destination.

A few minutes later at McDonald's my mum brought me a tray with my burger and chips on it and slid it over the table to me.

I pushed it back, saying I wasn't hungry. Mum asked me what was wrong and I explained. I can't remember exactly what I said but I can still feel the way I felt - sick in my stomach, from the injustice of that homeless man having nothing to eat, while we were so easily feasting on food.

Mum then slid her tray to the side, leaned over the table and started talking to me. She empathised that this was a sad situation. She then went on to tell me that, sadly, this is reality and there are other homeless people on other streets I had not yet seen. She commented on the system, telling me there were safety nets in society that are meant to catch and help people in need but sometimes it fails. She also suggested we could help them ourselves in different ways, but to take care when offering money as it might be used in ways harmful to the homeless person. We talked about how food is normally a good way of helping, and she suggested "What if we bought an extra burger on our way out of McDonald's and gave it to the man?" So we did just that.

This conversation with mum is something I will always remember. I don't remember word for word what she said, but I do remember the way she made me feel. How she helped me process the sensation of feeling sick and sad, to understand better what was going on and what we could do about it.

All this through a five-minute conversation.

Communication is a meta-skill

"Communication is such an important skill, it's one thing to be really creative or analytical, but if you can't communicate your thoughts and ideas then you won't be as effective."

These were the words of Neha, a friend of mine who is an Assistant Principal at an OFSTED Outstanding school in the

UK. Their values are built on hard work, integrity and honesty and their academic scores are in the top 1% across the country.

I see it the same way.

Consider a workplace you know well. What do people there do on a daily basis to work well and succeed? Likely there will be lots of talking and emailing and presenting, all forms of communication we hope our children become proficient at also.

Communication is a meta-skill, one of the essential gateways by which we can be good at other stuff.

Here are three ways in which good communication skills can build other important skills in our children.

1. Confidence - we encourage kids to use their voice and get used to being heard. We confirm their opinion is worth hearing and encourage them to speak their truths.
2. Empathy - we teach our kids to listen and understand others. We also show our kids how to listen and improve their interpersonal skills.
3. Critical thinking and resilience - conversations allow us to be exposed to different viewpoints, and we can show our kids how to navigate disagreements or different points of view in a healthy way.

Little things can become big things

When I speak to parenting experts about encouraging more conversations with kids they are always incredibly supportive.

It won't surprise you to hear they value the family connection and bonding that can emerge from a simple conversation.

Something I was also pleasantly surprised to discover is how little causal chats can pave the way for big important conversations when needed.

As parenting expert Ariadne Brill says at Positive Parenting Connection: "Conversations build connection. When children feel connected to their parents, they are more likely to feel well and be cooperative. The more our children feel they can talk to us about the little things, the more likely they will be to open up about the bigger issues later on."[1]

It turns out if children know the lines of dialogue are open, they are more likely to use them about something important should it be necessary.

So if you are regularly having fast and fun chats about aliens, football or even Harry Potter then you are more likely to have your child come to you if something more serious has happened or if they are worried about anything.

Expert Insights:
Sue Atkins - BBC, Disney Family & ITV This Morning parenting expert[3]

From the moment your toddler asks "Why?" they are curious about the world and how it works. As parents we can encourage and nurture this curiosity in the natural conversations we have on a regular basis with our children as they grow and mature: on the way to school, in the car, on the way to swimming lessons or walking the dog. The opportunities are endless and are only limited by your imagination.

Conversations are supposed to be fun. They involve the personal interactions between you and your child about something of interest, yet many parents worry about having conversations with their kids. They are concerned they won't be able to keep the conversation going, or they don't feel confident in using conversation as magic moments of informal learning - what I call 'talking and teaching' opportunities. The approach laid out in this book takes away that anxiety.

The first and most important rule of conversation is it is not all about you, but it's not all about your child either. It's what Hirsh-Pasek and Roberta Golinkoff refer to as a "conversational duet."[4]

A monologue, in either direction, is not conversation. That's why the questions in this book inspire different conversations and take them away from the usual family conversations of nagging about eating broccoli, doing homework, or putting shoes away - into the magic of exploring, laughing, chatting and being playful together. The questions are so interesting as they act as the spark to ignite different ways of thinking and communicating naturally through the ebb and flow of conversation.

Through simply asking out of the box questions and interacting together you can quickly, easily, and inexpensively develop your child's creativity, critical thinking, resilience, communication, leadership and confidence.

But I do this already

Right now you may be thinking I am stating the obvious.

Of course conversations matter. Of course I should be talking to my kids. Of course I want to build memories and skills at the same time.

If so, that's great.

But are you asking the right questions leading to the right types of conversation?

It turns out we parents often narrow down the scope of the possible conversation, without intending to. There is a bit of a trick though in how we can ask questions to open things up.

If this sounds intriguing then turn that page, because that is exactly what we will cover in part B.

PART B: WHAT?

CHAPTER 4

What types of questions will help my kids build the skills they need?

"Good questions inform. Great questions transform."

Ken Coleman - Career Coach

What's 2+2? If you answered 4 then you are right. You get full marks and go to the top of the class.

If only real life had answers that were so clear cut. In reality, we all know the world is not as black and white as this and we often have to think in the 'grey space.'

It turns out asking open-ended questions where there is no right answer is one of the best things you can do to help your child appreciate this.

Feed their curiosity

But why mum? But why dad?

Do you remember all those *Why?* questions your children have asked you over the years? Maybe they still do. I was the same and I bet you were when you were younger too. It's just in our DNA.

All humans are born curious.

The problem is the 'system' somehow filters this out of us at a young age. Education systems tend to focus on the 'right answer' and I don't blame them. It is much easier to test someone on whether they know what 2+2 is and grade them accordingly, rather than test them somehow on their creativity, critical thinking or empathy levels.

I was recently speaking to an education expert in this space. His view was the 'peak' question age of children is about four years old. After that children tend to ask fewer questions and coincidentally this is about the age many start school.

How sad is that?

I think we all want to keep our kids curious and learning about the world, and encourage them to keep asking good questions. The role we play at home goes a long way in supporting this.

Expert Insights:
Dr Lani Watson - University of Oxford, Co-Founder of The Questioning Strengths Method[1]

Questioning is so familiar and ubiquitous, it's easy to forget it's also a skill we had to learn, just like walking, counting, and reading. Arguably, we learn to question before we even start talking, when we first reach out with a curious hand to touch something unfamiliar and find out what it feels like (or tastes like). From there, we learn to ask all sorts of questions about our environment and the people we share it with. These questions are essential for learning and development.

As we get older, questions often start to fade into the background. Education typically orients us, slowly but surely, towards providing answers, rather than asking questions and so we develop our answering rather than asking skills. By the time we are adults in the workplace, most of us will have spent very little, if any, time focusing explicitly on our ability to ask great questions. For many, this powerful but underdeveloped skill goes unnoticed.

Children, on the other hand, ask many unexpected and challenging questions and typically love to be challenged with questions too. That's why learning to ask the right questions is not only an effective way to get great conversations going with children but also a fantastic way to reignite your own questioning skills as an adult. A win-win for everyone.

In my experience, doing philosophy with children in schools, some of the best questions are the ones that seem easy to answer at first but can easily turn into exciting and engaged debate once kids realise not everyone thinks the same way. These questions can unlock sustained and often impressively sophisticated philosophical thinking.

So, when you are thinking up great questions to start interesting and memorable conversations with your kids, remember you are developing and practicing your own skills as a questioner too. Just be sure to leave enough time for their questions in return.

Avoid transactional talk

As a parent or caregiver you are in a unique position, being able to ask your kids a bunch of questions and genuinely nurture their inquisitive side. But it's way too easy to slip into what I call 'transactional talk.' The kind of quick questions or statements that busy, time-poor parents often slip into (me included).

These transactional questions sound like:

- *Have you done your homework?*
- *What did you eat for lunch?*
- *Is your bag packed for tomorrow?*
- *Is your room tidy?*

Or my personal favourite, which always leads to a dead-end, yet I can't help but keep asking:

- *How was school today?*

Any question that can be answered with a "Yes", "No", "Fine", or "OK" answer will surely have just that mumbled back at us.

But what if we asked a zany, quirky and sideways question? Something your child would not expect? When was the last time you tried that?

Questions with no right answers

The questions I champion are open-ended questions. These are questions that don't have a right or wrong answer. They are much better for kids' brains because they actually need to think about what they think.

So what is an open-ended question?

Well, let's say your child is into football.

Some closed-ended questions might be:

- *Who invented football?*
- *How many players are there on a pitch?*
- *What is the offside rule?*
- *Do you like football?*
- *What position do you play?*

Each of these could be answered with a fact or a one-word answer, and don't lend themselves to a continuation of dialogue.

Open-ended questions in contrast might be:

- *How would you explain football to an alien?*
- *What are the strengths and weaknesses of your favourite team?*
- *What new rule could you invent for football?*
- *Should footballers be paid more than nurses?*
- *If your team was losing at half-time what would you say in the dressing room to your teammates?*

Each of these will require a few sentences in reply and original thought. None of them have a right answer.

It doesn't matter how they explain football, what new rule they invent or what their inspirational team talk sounds like. The point is your kids will get practice at talking and thinking on the spot and have a chance to form and share their opinion.

It's so refreshing and kids love it.

If you want to come up with more questions like this just ask yourself: "What's a question with no right answer?"

Pause for a moment right now, and see what you can come up with.

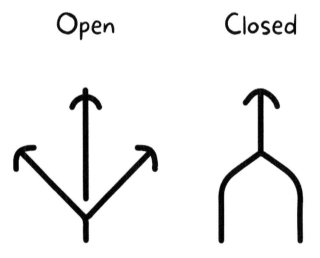

Open   Closed

Fig 4: Two Type of Questions

Using questions to build specific skills

The other way I often think about good questions to ask is to pick a certain skill I know I want to build in my kids.

I'll illustrate by picking the skills critical thinking, creativity and empathy. See if you can satisfy yourself that each of the examples I suggest is open-ended and could be answered in multiple ways.

Critical Thinking

Critical thinking is a form of problem solving or logical reasoning. As the world's information becomes ever more commoditised, using critical thinking when we make decisions is increasingly important.

A question that builds critical thinking might encourage children to explore pros and cons, examining topics from both sides and multiple perspectives before coming up with their own balanced opinion, e.g. *Would chocolate rain be good or bad?*

Another method is to require some form of categorisation, ordering or prioritisation of elements. The brain workout is in the trade-offs required to move things up or down the list, e.g. *What three things would you take with you to a desert island?*

Or you could go with open-ended *What if?* question that invites your child to think about what the result could be of the creative hypothetical you are mentioning. Here the emphasis is on sequential thinking about what happens next, e.g. *What would the world be like if money didn't exist?*

Creativity

Creativity builds the left part of our brains. It allows us to view problems from a different angle, be more innovative and overall more open-minded, something that is highly valued in society.

We are trying to stimulate the imagination so we can have loads of fun here, using topics kids are interested in. Perhaps if your child is into arts and crafts you could ask a colour question, e.g. *What would you call a new colour that you invent?*

For any parent familiar with creative writing you'll know English teachers like you to use all your senses when describing something. You can do the same when asking for a verbal response, e.g. *If aliens exist, what might they be like?*

Finally, one of my favourite hacks is to come up with multiple uses for any object around the house. When the obvious ones are exhausted you can physically feel the brain firing as it tries to come up with even wackier ideas, e.g. *What are 10 things we can do with a sock?*

Empathy

Not only does building empathy mean our kids will do better in their interpersonal relationships, but it's also a chance to check on their mental health.

Empathy based questions look more like an exploration of feelings and situations. They are very people-based, focusing on emotions rather than logic.

Perspective-taking is important here. Ask your child to empathise with someone else (a relative, a friend or even a character in a movie) and then ask things like *How are they feeling?* or *What could we do to cheer them up?*

You can also have a more existential chat about the wider roles of feelings and emotions. This helps to validate their place and make even big, scary emotions feel safe, e.g. *What would happen if no one had any feelings?* or *Can bad feelings ever be good?*

For a parent with a child who is struggling with something themselves, you can also turn them into a fictitious counsellor for someone else. This could help them come up with good strategies for managing their own emotions, e.g. *If your friend was nervous to go to a party, what would you say to them?*

Discuss books

We all know the importance of reading to our kids.

For a reading session that is going well, where your child is really into the book, you might consider extending your time by just five minutes at the end to ask some thoughtful questions.

Take a look at a few of these examples. Each is open-ended and builds the skill in brackets.

- *How would you summarise the plot in less than a minute?* (Communication)
- *What three other titles would have worked well for this book?* (Creativity)
- *Which is better and why - the book or the movie?* (Critical Thinking)
- *What are the key strengths and weaknesses of this character?* (Empathy)
- *What description could you write on the back to promote this book?* (Communication)

Do you see how these are very different to the usual comprehension questions your kids are probably used to? Normally after reading a book children have to answer questions factually based on the passage of text. When you are having a 'Little Big' conversation at home, however, you get to open the dialogue up and feed their curiosity and creativity.

Talking about the news

The news is a goldmine of conversational opportunities.

There are always multiple perspectives you can take and the topics are always about issues that matter. Getting your kids talking and thinking about the news has the added benefit of encouraging them to be active global citizens.

Imagine it's Wednesday and you are watching the news together. There is a story about some recent lottery winners who have splashed the cash and ended up bankrupt after just one year. Oh dear. You could talk about how silly they are, but you see it as a coaching moment to develop critical thinking skills instead.

So you start to talk about money and playing the lottery, e.g. *Why did those people play the lottery? How have their feelings changed since they won and then lost the cash? What would you do with £100m of winnings?*

This approach can work for nearly any news story you happen to watch on the TV - try it out next time.

I find the best news-related questions are those about people, e.g. *What would you do in that situation? How might they be feeling? What might they do next?* These are usually good prompts.

One note of caution is that the news can be a bit serious and grown-up at times. So you may wish to look at certain sites for child-friendly news topics. There is a site by the Guardian that has a nice list of different resources which I frequently check and is linked to in the notes at the back of this book.[2] One thing I notice with many kids' sites like this however is, while the news story itself is well-written, the formulation of discussion questions is hit and miss.

That's why I take the time to write a news-related discussion card in the KidCoachApp regularly. I read around and write down a quick summary of something interesting that happened in the week and then spend time crafting juicy discussion questions and prompts you can directly use.

Parent Stories:

Alison - mum of eight year old

I work at a technology company and my husband is a computer programmer. I first came across this approach in early 2021 and it has been revolutionary for us.

I always want to be having conversations that matter with my kids but it is hard when I'm tired at the end of the day. As parents, there are only so many conversations we can think of.

I love referencing a massive library of skills and prompts. That makes it so much easier to keep these conversations going. It has helped so much with that moment when you all sit down for dinner and want to have a meaningful conversation. I find so much value in this as it enables me to enjoy the conversation with my child and not have to think on my feet all the time. Sometimes you just need some inspiration.

It has made my son more talkative for sure - in the car, at dinner and all around the house. It has really improved his social skills and he opens up more when talking about other things as a family too. It is also making a difference in the way our family communicates. We have figured out when we talk together best.

Fig 5: Lunch Atop A Skyscraper
(reproduced here under creative commons license)

Use images and pictures

If a picture paints a thousand words then we can probably come up with hundreds of questions about them.

Our children will see pictures all the time - in books, magazines, art, billboards and even cereal packaging. We can also look for specific pictures online and come up with a raft of curious questions about them.

To illustrate, take a look at the iconic 'Lunch Atop a Skyscraper' image just above.[3] It's the black-and-white image of 11 construction workers eating lunch while sitting on a steel beam high up in New York city in 1932.

Consider asking your children:

- *What do you think they are eating?* (Creativity)
- *Why are some smiling and others not?* (Empathy)
- *What might they be talking about?* (Creativity)
- *Are they safe?* (Critical Thinking)
- *Would this happen nowadays?* (Philosophy)
- *What questions do you have about the picture?* (Critical Thinking)

Questions like this support communication skills (to describe what they see), creativity skills (imagining what else is going on), critical thinking skills (querying why this is happening) and much more.

What questions will you come up with the next time you see an interesting image?

50 more questions your kids will love

By now you will be getting the sense there are so many juicy questions for kids we can come up with, if we are thinking along the right lines. It can be hard to do on the spot of course. At the end of a long and busy day at work, our brains can struggle to be creative and innovative.

That's why I've jotted down more questions for you to use at the back of this book. Appendix II has 50 questions your kids will love to talk and think about, and should help you on one of those days when it is tricky to come up with something on the fly.

Any one of these questions could be the start of a wonderful conversation, with some lovely back and forths. It does require the follow-up prompts to be just as good as the initial question, however, and is what we are going to take a look at next.

CHAPTER 5

What are ways I can help my child think more broadly and more deeply?

"The important thing is not to stop questioning."

Albert Einstein

Hopefully by now you are getting the gist of what I am so passionate about and you can see yourself starting up some conversations like this.

If so, you might be wondering how to continue the dialogue once it gets going?

Kids are notorious for giving one word answers, flatly stating "I don't know" or just running off to the next distraction. So how can you keep their attention with thought-provoking prompts, which also help your kids think more broadly and more deeply?

That is how the magic really happens. Getting into rich two way conversations is not only fantastic for getting talking and thinking practice, but is also what makes the moment stick in the mind and become a cherished memory for all.

In this chapter I will walk you through a handful of classic prompting questions which nearly always work. Let's assume you had opened with *Would you like to live forever?* which is an excellent conversation starter.

Here is how you could continue the conversation.

What could happen next?

This helps children think about the consequences of whatever we are talking about. It encourages them to slow down and not rush an idea, response or action. It encourages them to be thoughtful about the intention of what they are doing.

Example: *If you lived forever what would you do with the time?*

Maybe they would like it filled with games, fun and friends. Or maybe it could get boring and so living forever becomes a disadvantage. Thinking forwards gives more information about whether they would actually want to live forever or not.

Can you give me an example?

This helps make vague notions much more concrete. It is good practice to talk in examples as it makes you far better understood by others when telling a story or trying to communicate a message. Kids also love it when you ask them something very specific about their life.

Example: *What's the first thing you would do if you could live forever?*

Maybe they would start saving money. Maybe they would want to stop working. Maybe they want to get very fit and healthy. Or maybe it would be something totally unexpected. Examples are such an effective way of peeking inside our children's minds.

When has this happened before?

This encourages children to look for historic patterns or evidence we already have. Maybe they tried this particular thing themselves when they were younger. Maybe they have learnt from history about something similar. Maybe it happened in a movie they watched and they learned it that way.

Example: *Somebody tried to live forever in Harry Potter - what happened there?*

This will make sense to Harry Potter fans. In the first book they find the Philosopher's Stone, which has special powers to let their owner live forever. Fights break out to claim ownership of the stone and it requires a very noble Harry to come and save the day. Would similar fights break out if something like this existed in real life?

Who can we ask for more ideas?

When figuring anything out we don't need to do it ourselves. We can go out and ask someone, ideally a range of people who are familiar with the situation and who might have varied views. Sometimes the mere thought exercise of taking someone else's perspective will give you more ideas anyway.

Example: *What would your 80 year old Grandma say to this?*

Here we deliberately consider the view of someone who is probably nearing the end of their life, not at the beginning of life like your child would be. Would Grandma love to keep living? Or is she happy with the life she has had? Are her thoughts representative of all old people?

Expert Insights:
Topsy Page - Talk and Philosophy for Children specialist[1]

I work with schools to develop a culture of high quality dialogue and reasoning across the curriculum. I believe high quality talk is a vital ingredient in narrowing the gap and improving outcomes.

It starts at home. Talking develops your child's confidence, ideas, reasoning, and ability to work with others. It can also contribute to improved reading and writing.

To get your children interested in talking you can ask open, thought-provoking or funny questions e.g. *Would you rather eat cold gravy or fried ants? What would you do if you had a magic wand? Should people have to pay for food? What would you do if you were in charge of the world? What if animals could talk?"*

Develop their listening and responding skills by saying things like *Ooh, that's interesting, did you hear what Isha just said? Do you agree/disagree? Why? What do you think about what Davey said? Can you add a bit more to your Mum's idea? Who can explain what Dad means when he says that? Why do you think your brother said that?* Make it into a game, e.g. touch your nose if you can repeat what your sister just said.

Remember to offer lots of specific praise like *I love the way you're thinking it through. Great – you listened really well, Annie. Thanks for disagreeing calmly, Benito. I like the way you've asked a question. That's really making me think.* (instead of *Well done, Good girl* etc.)

For your youngest children not talking much yet you can still develop language. Just comment lots on play or actions e.g. *You're rolling the ball. Rolling the red ball. You've picked up the ball. Oops. You dropped the ball.* Just put into words what they're doing. Don't ask questions or expect them to respond. Try to do at least 20 minutes a day 'commenting'.

My top tips for parents are to:

- Make sure you genuinely listen to your child's thoughts and ideas. Don't guess what they're going to say or finish their sentences.
- Set aside some daily time for talking, e.g. teatime.
- Don't push if they aren't in the mood for talking. Wait for something that sparks their interest. Then listen.

What would your friends say to this?

We shouldn't follow a majority or consensus all the time, but if most people feel a certain way it is probably important to find out why. Taking other people's perspectives, even as a thought experiment, is a good way to think about an old problem in a new way.

Example: *How many of your classmates would say yes or no?*

Your child could actually go out and poll them. Or it might be enough to think about a few close friends and consider what they would say. Ask your child this and maybe they will come up tomorrow with lots of ideas you didn't talk about today.

What's the best question you can ask here?

You know you are having a good conversation when your child starts asking juicy questions themselves. It is a clear signal they are interested, engaged and thinking deeply about the topic. It also levels the playing field so we are not always the "question master." In a traditional school classroom, the teacher is usually the one asking most of the questions, so this is a way to make the home learning feel very different.

Example: *What questions could you ask about the offer to live forever before you decide?*

The original question was so open it was crying out for some clarifications. When trying this with children myself these are some of the questions they have come up with: *Will I always be healthy? Can my family live forever too? Can I change my mind whenever I want?* Great questions.

How can you test your answer?

As important as it is to think clearly in our heads, it is just as important to try things out and react to what happens. We can encourage our children to adopt this mindset with anything, such as trying to learn the piano for a few months, or trying a new food they haven't come across yet.

Example: *How could you test if you will like this?*

Before deciding to live forever you could always ask to try it out for a while before making your mind up. You could also go and speak to 10 really old people to see what they would say, and whether they would recommend you to take this offer up.

Having thought about this some more, do you want to change your mind?

This is good to ask towards the end of the discussion. After five or 10 minutes of talking, your brains have been nicely warmed up and you have probably looked at the problem from many sides. At this point they might have started to feel differently from their first gut response. That's OK. Thoughtful mind-changing should be encouraged. You shouldn't stick to opinions just to save face or because your ego won't let you yield.

Example: *There seem to be quite a few disadvantages to living forever. Are you sure you don't want to change your mind?*

Maybe the live forever conversation brought up issues of ill health for a long time, or of missing friends and family that can't be with you, or just of sheer boredom and running out of stuff to do. In that case it is a healthy practice to actually change your mind from a yes to a no, as long as your child can back up why they are doing so.

Parent stories:
Sonya - mum of nine and 12 year old

I took a break from my project management career and trained to become a children's coach.

As someone who is passionate about emotional intelligence and social etiquette, I love questions encouraging confidence, resilience, and empathy. My favourite question is *What kind act could we do for someone else this week?*

Taking a questioning approach helps me turn those mundane moments into meaningful opportunities. It supports my child's critical thinking skills for any philosophical or moral questions.

I like the fact my children are now evaluating the world and how things work on a deeper level. They are acquiring skills to help them with academia and future career skills such as communication, leadership and teamwork.

Mindset matters

Don't worry if you are struggling to remember these sorts of prompting questions. Your mindset and attitude matters far more.

If you are curious and thoughtful, comfortable with the ambiguity of the topic and happy to think through the topic together with your child - then you will find everything just flows.

You don't need to be asking perfectly curated questions every time. Just go with it. Keep the verbal tennis rally going. Change tack to cover new ground when you sense it is running out of material. Be silly and keep it all fun.

You can do it.

A conversation I will always remember

A few summers ago we took the kids to Centre Parcs (a forest and activity camp in the UK). One day I took my eldest daughter, Mia, out for a walk.

I was in a chatty mood and thought I would try out some more of these questions I was getting into the swing of asking. It turned into one of those awesome conversations that tacked in different directions.

It was equal parts silly and serious, had lots of why and what do you think type nudges, and used the environment of trees and animals around us to stimulate thinking. I jotted down some notes immediately afterwards and was able to write the full dialogue soon after.

I'd love to share it with you here as I think it nicely illustrates how the right questions can turn a conversation from good to great.

[We started by walking into the woods.]

Me: So Mia, who do you think made these paths?

Mia: I don't know

Me: Me neither...but who do you think?

Mia: Erm, probably the first people to walk here.

Me: Yeah, probably. I wonder what would it be like to be an explorer. Imagine what it would feel like to be the first person to ever go somewhere.

Mia: It would be scary.

Me: Scary...why?

Mia: Because you don't know what will be there.

Me: True. But you also get to make it your own place and set your own laws.

Mia: Like rules?

Me: Yes, exactly. What 3 rules would you make if you found a new country?

[We stopped to listen to some animal sounds in the trees.]

Mia: What animal is that?

Me: I'm not sure. What do you think?

Mia: I think it's a Gruffalo.

Me: Haha, well, maybe it is. Or maybe it's a lion.

Mia: Don't be a silly daddy. Lions don't live in trees.

Me: Well, why not? It's nice and cosy, and there are plenty of mice to eat.

Mia: Because lions need to run around lots – they need more space.

Me: Ah, OK. Like our garden maybe? Shall we get a lion as a pet?

Mia: No, people only have dogs and cats as pets, nobody has lions.

Me: Why not? They could keep you safe from bad people, right?

Mia: Because they're too loud.

Me: Loud? Is that the only reason? Why else do people not keep lions as pets?

Mia: Because they could eat you.

Me: Ha. That's true. Law of nature some would say. You know - some people eat animals. Do you think that's OK?

Mia: Yup. We eat fish sometimes.

Me: Fair enough. So what about dogs and cats – why don't we eat them?

Mia: Aww, they're too cute to eat.

Me: So should how cute something is affect how we treat it? What about humans – should we treat a pretty person better?

[Heading back to lodge now.]

Mia: I'm tired now.

Me: Me too. Shall we go for ice cream then?

Mia: Yes, let's go.

Me: Ah, so you're not too tired to keep walking then?

Mia: Erm, well I do want ice cream...

Me: The only thing that changed was me talking about ice cream – how does that suddenly make you not tired?

Mia: Erm...

Me: Perhaps it is something to do with your mindset.

Mia: What's a mindset?

Me: Mindset is just a way of thinking about things, and choosing what you want to feel. For instance, I could choose to feel tired because I want to sit down. Or I could choose to have energy because I want to go for ice cream.

Mia: OK...

Me: So what's another example of this?

Mia: I don't know.

Me: What's another situation where your feelings change because of something you are looking forward to?

Mia: Umm, like when I get to watch TV after I have done my homework?

Me: Yes, exactly. It's good to have things to look forward to, isn't it? Having rewards is a great way of getting things done.

Mia: Is it the only way?

Me: Probably not. Let's think together. How else would you motivate someone to get something done?

Mia: Like what the Sun did instead of the Wind in that story...

To this day I remember this conversation well enough I can write it down like this. I don't think I will ever forget it and I hope Mia doesn't either.

Did these examples help?

How was that? Did it help? Can you see yourself using these nudging prompts to keep conversations going? Can you also see yourself coming up with a few depending on where your child steers the conversation?

I hope so.

It's these sort of continuation prompts that often make or break a good conversation. It helps the dialogue go back and forth, and helps us take the conversation from side to side as we help our children explore the topic from all angles.

As you have more of these types of conversations you will probably think of your own prompts that make sense and work for your situation and your kids. I really encourage you to do this. Parents who have been doing this for a while report they seem to be generating a knack for coming up with well-worded prompts themselves.

If you find yourself using my app and coming up with juicy prompts that we hadn't thought of then I'd love to hear what it was. Just send me an email at hello@kidcoach.app.

There are also some generic prompts that nearly always work listed in Appendix IV. I encourage you to scan through them and perhaps even jot a few down on post-it notes as you are getting used to this new approach.

CHAPTER 6

What do conversations with other children sound like?

"Conversation is like a dance. Taking turns, following and leading."

Loren Ekroth - Founder of Better Conversations

Parents sometimes message me and say, "These are great questions, but what's the right answer?" However, the point is there is no right answer. That's what makes the questions so good in the first place.

Still, I understand the question. Sometimes you just need to know where you are headed or what a "good" conversation sounds like. These types of conversations with kids are different, so I appreciate it could help to hear some illustrative responses.

100+ conversations with kids

That's why I started our podcast Questions To Ask Your Kids.[1] It's where I have the pleasure of talking to lots of different children, asking them lots of juicy questions and getting into quick, fun and thought-provoking chats with all of them. 100+ and counting.

Each episode is a 10-15 minute recording of a child who is six to 12 years old answering questions from our app. It has helped us test out some of our questions and improve them where needed, as well as being super fun to do.

The main purpose of the podcast though is to help parents like you hear what real-life conversations and children's responses could sound like. You are more than welcome to search for 'Questions To Ask Your Kids' in your usual podcast player and, if you do, I recommend you hit the subscribe/follow button to ensure you always get the latest instalment.

Let's take a look at some highlights of conversations that were designed to build certain skills. I've written down some dialogues, each starting with a KidCoach question and each of which illustrate a unique approach.

Confidence: reminding of what they have already accomplished and how

Me: What do you find easy that was once hard?

Bobby (9 years old): Maths, running and jumping and not being able to carry heavy stuff.

Me: Tell me about running, why was that hard for you?

Bobby: I couldn't sprint as much, I was sometimes really slow. Once I kept on training I got faster.

Me: Why did you keep trying and not give up?

Bobby: Because I wanted to beat people and run faster in races.

Me: Right, because you wanted to win the race. So even though it hurt a little bit and even though it's a bit difficult you kept going yeah?

Bobby: Yep

Me: That's amazing I love that, and tell me about maths, why did you find that hard?

Bobby: Because I didn't know my times table in Year 2 and I didn't know what the answer was and eventually I learnt it and now I'm faster at my times tables.

Me: What changed? How did you get better?

Bobby: My legs got stronger.

Me: For running yeah, but what about maths?

Bobby: I wanted to keep on trying and I eventually got past my 3 times tables and 2s and I am all the way up to my 9s now and 10s and 12s.

Me: Wow, getting into the big numbers now. What mindset was the most helpful in overcoming the difficulties in learning your times tables?

Bobby: Well, I did the tuition with my auntie, and she helped me a little bit better. And I always had help doing them. They kept moving me up to different times tables and I eventually got used to them and got to learn them really quickly.

Me: That's great, so you got someone to help you and did you want her to help you?

Bobby: Yep.

Me: That's great. Because sometimes not everybody wants or realises they need help.

Critical Thinking: evaluating pros and cons (of robot arms)

Me: If you could have a robot arm would you have one?

Stephen (10 years old): Well, on one side I would have to have an operation to get this arm installed. But on the positive side, I could be a lot more precise with what I wanted to do. If I wanted to pick up something very small then I could very easily do that if I could be precise...because obviously, robots could be a lot more precise than humans can.

Me: What are some advantages of a robot arm?

Stephen: Well with a robot arm you could have a watch fitted on it. You can have loads of applications on it to tell you various things like the time instead of having a watch. You could have a heartbeat reader.

Me: Would you actually want to be a robot?

Stephen: No, because then you wouldn't have any unique talent. Because then you would just be this average robot. Because say you could do something very special as a human, but say if you couldn't do that as a human then you would basically just be a robot. And if all your body parts were replaced, then you wouldn't be a human anymore you would just be a walking robot and you wouldn't be able to do what you could previously do as a human such as I don't know... I have a coding talent, if I wanted to make a particular programme the robot may not know what particular programme to make.

Creativity: taking something they mention and drilling into it for more ideas

Me: What are 10 different things you can do with a cup?

Aziza (9 years old): You can fill it with water and drink it, you can get lots of different cups and build things. If it's really hot you can fill the cup up with water again and pour it over your head, and you can build towers, and you can get a stick and turn the cup upside down and play the drums in it.

Me: So stay on that stream of thought, you can build and stack and you can turn it upside down and play the drums with it, what other things can you do with the cup upside down?

Aziza: Hmm, you can...ermmm...You can put toys and things that you can stand on it. You can erm... OH. You can trace around it.

Me: What was that last one?

Aziza: You can get a pencil and trace around it.

Me: Yeah brilliant. I definitely wouldn't have thought of that...

Critical Thinking: thinking about all the details

Me: If you were planning a party, what do you need to prepare?

Amaya (11 years old): So you need to think about location, firstly. If it's all of your friends, I have quite a lot of friends and I don't think my house will be big enough so I might get a kind of hall somewhere. Or in the garden, depending on the weather. You need to think about food because obviously you can't have a party without food and you need to think about decorations, how you are gonna make it look. You are gonna need to think about music and activities. I think it depends on the weather because you don't want it raining when you are outside.

Me: What about catering to everyone's needs, what do you need to prepare?

Amaya: Oh yeah, the food. you need to make sure that people don't have allergies and you need to cater to the allergies because yeah. You need to make sure the food's nice and everyone likes it... like pizza.

Fig 7: What A Good Conversation Looks Like

Communication: asking about the differences between things

Me: How would you describe a car to an alien?

Millie (7 year old): Well first to an alien, I would say that a car is something that you can get in and move around to different places faster than you can walk. Erm, then I would say and talk to him about the steering wheel and the first thing I would say when I showed him the car is to tell him it's a car, otherwise, he could think that it's something else.

Me: Wow, so I love that answer, Millie. So you talked about three different, but all really important things. Right, so first of all you said this is a car so you put a label on it. Then you also talked about why you need a car and then you started describing what it looks like, the steering and the turning of the car. Which is brilliant. I'd love for you to continue that, what are other ways you can describe a car? Because if I was an alien I might think that a bicycle is a car because bicycles are quicker than walking, bicycles have something you can steer to turn and bicycles have wheels. So how can you keep telling me about cars to make it really clear in my head what a car is?

Millie: I'd say that a car has a foot pedal and if you press the foot pedal and steering wheel it will go, and if you take your foot off the foot pedal and steering wheel it will stop.

Me: Okay but it could be a quad bike...

Millie: I'd also say that a car is in the shape of a semicircle and it has four wheels, erm and it has two at the front and two at the back and I'd also tell them that a car has seats and I haven't seen a car with one seat.

Me: Okay, very good description. Yeah, probably just racing cars have one seat. So what do cars make you feel?

Empathy: trying to find the words to describe a feeling

Me: What do you think friendship is?

Zac (7 years old): I think it's when you like people and can believe in them and you can tell someone to do something and ensure they do it.

Me: What do you mean by someone you can believe in?

Zac: Well you believe that you know they will do something that you ask them to do.

Me: If I think about this like an alien, someone who I believe will do something for me. Hmm like someone who works for me?

Zac: It's someone who is kind to you and does stuff kind to you.

Me: Okay so it's about kindness then?

Zac: Yeah.

Me: Okay are friends always people who are kind to you?

Zac: No, it's sometimes people who like to play football with you and believe in you.

Me: Okay, there are a few things that make friends, friends. Can you maybe give me five words you think are the five things that make a friend?

Zac: Erm, kindness and I can't really think of any other words but I can think of stuff to do with them.

Me: Okay no problem, that's fine, let's do five things that will show that someone is your friend.

Zac: Okay they can be kind to you and believe in you and they like you.

Me: Good start, can you think of two more?

Zac: Hmm...

Me: It is tricky isn't it, five words to describe a friend. So I am going to ask you that question in a little bit and see if you have any more answers okay?

Zac: Okay.

Me: So does it matter how long you have been friends? Are you better friends with someone you've known for three years or three months?

Zac: What did you say?

Me: Does it matter how long you have been friends? Are you better friends with someone you've known for three years or three months?

Zac: Not really

Me: How so?

Zac: Well you are friends with someone who is kind to you, but all the time. It doesn't matter how long you have been with them.

Me: Okay so it matters how you spend your time together not how long you have known them.

Zac: ...It just matters if they are kind to you and if they believe in you.

Me: Okay that's good, these are very good solid points and three key bits that make a friend.

Critical Thinking: making comparisons and giving reasons

Me: I want to ask a question about the past and future. Who do you think had the better life, your generation or your grandparent's generation? You and your siblings or your grandparents?

Dan (7 years old): Me and my siblings, because I think that back then there was war and not a lot of things to use and it would just be harder. And, and, and a lot of years ago cars didn't even have seatbelts and it would be really dangerous.

Me: What other ways was their way of life not as good?

Dan: We probably have more fun technology which they might not have had. Like the Nintendo switch, they probably did not have that

Me: No they probably didn't have Nintendo Switch at all no haha.

Numbers: being clear on the amounts of things talked about

Me: So Luan, you are really into coding.

Luan (9 years old): Uh huh, a lot.

Me: So I was thinking, what are the steps you need to make a jam sandwich, if you were to code the instructions to make a jam sandwich what would you write?

Luan: I would write... Do you want me to say it in code or do you want me to say it in real life?

Me: That's a really good clarifying question but for now let's do real life, maybe later we can think about it in code.

Luan: I would say go to the shops and then buy tons of ingredients.

Me: Tons of ingredients okay.

Luan: Then go back home and then erm and then say get some bread and then stack it until they are both on top of each other, and put some ingredients underneath, I mean between them and then eat it.

Me: Great I love that you started by going to the shops and not assuming it's in the fridge... you mentioned we need tons of ingredients, should we take a massive lorry, do you literally mean tonnes of ingredients?

Luan: Yeah I would say 100 of each ingredient.

Me: To make a jam sandwich?

Luan: Yeah (silence) because I want to make a jam sandwich for life.

Me: Ahhh I see, haha amazing. If you want to make a lot of jam sandwiches, give me a number. How many do you want to make?

Luan: 500.

Me: I see you need a lot of bread and jam then, erm are they going to go off?

Parent stories:

David - dad of two young children

I'm a Partner at a global consulting company. It's a busy job but I do everything I can to spend quality time with my two daughters.

I wanted to find a way to keep my kids engaged and entertained while in the car. On longer drives our kids always fall asleep, which makes bedtime very challenging. So I was looking at audiobooks and podcasts to have them listen to, when I came across your questions. I liked how this would help me spend more meaningful time with them. So I gave it a go.

The best time to have these chats is in the car. I'm always dropping the kids off to school and we have a 25 min commute time. I will always pull up a question I like before we set off, so I have it in my head for the journey.

This method helps us be more intentional with our time with the kids. We now have a way to develop how our kids think.

My daughter asked me the other day when I picked her up from school, 'What questions are we going to discuss today?' It's become part of our daily routine as a family.

Spontaneous conversations with my own kids

Now, I know some of these dialogues you've just seen might seem a bit scripted. To be fair they were in the context of a 'coaching call' where we proactively sat down to discuss one of the questions I wrote.

You might choose to do that yourself, or you might have the opportunity to have more spontaneous chats.

There are times when we need to be reactive to what our child is saying or doing. But if we keep in our minds the skills we want to build and the types of questions and prompts that work, then we will be able to make the most of these opportunities when they arise.

You won't be surprised to hear I do this frequently at home with my kids. Especially with my eldest daughter, Mia. Each time we have one of those wonderful, spontaneous and thoughtful conversations I post it on Facebook to share with family and friends and also as a record for us to look back on.

Scrolling back through my feed now I wanted to share these real-life examples. Some are insightful and others are downright hilarious. Please bear in mind these are with a six year old.

Whether Goldilocks is naughty

Me: Goldilocks ran away when she was found. She didn't even say anything to the three bears.

Mia: No she didn't.

Me: What could she have said when they found her?

Mia: She could have said she is very tired and is it OK if they let her sleep for longer?

Me: She could have. Do you think they would have let her stay?

Mia: Maybe. Maybe Baby Bear would have wanted to play with her.

Me: Oh yes. I suppose she will never know. Because she didn't ask. She just ran away. Was that OK?

Mia: No.

Me: What should she have done?

Mia: Walked away. So she wouldn't trip.

Encouraging questions

Mia: My teacher drinks Coca Cola at lunchtime.

Me: Oh dear, will you tell her off?

Mia: I'm not allowed. She's a teacher.

Me: But you can ask her questions. Anybody can ask anybody questions.

Mia: Like telling her she shouldn't drink Coca Cola?

Me: Well, that's not a question. How would you make it a question?

Mia: I don't know.

Me: Don't say I don't know. Take a moment and think about it.

[Pauses.]

Mia: "Miss....is Coca Cola good for you?"

Me: Well done, that's a great question. What would she say in response?

Mia: "No."

Me: And what could you ask next?

Mia: "So why do you drink it?"

Having a conversation talking about boys and girls

Me: Would you like to be a boy?

Mia: Erm...yes.

Me: Interesting...all the time or just to try?

Mia: Just to try.

Me: It's good to try new things.

Mia: I'd do it for a day.

Me: Ooh, that would be an exciting day. What would you do?

Mia: Get messy.

Me: Hmm. OK. Why?

Mia: Because that's what boys do.

Me: OK...and what do girls do then?

Mia: Have lots of dresses and pretty things to put in their hair.

[Thinking about how to dispel gender stereotypes.]

Me: So at school do you have boys and girls in your class?

Mia: Yes

Me: And does your teacher treat you differently to boys?

Mia: Erm...no.

Me: Does she care if you are a boy or a girl?

Mia: No she doesn't care.

Me: So does it matter if you are a boy or a girl?

Mia: It's the same really.

Talking about magical powers and getting excited for Christmas

Mia: When I get my wishing well from Santa I'm going to wish for magical powers.

Me: That sounds fun. What would you do with them?

Mia: First, I'd freeze all of my teachers and everybody at school.

Me: Even your friends?

Mia: Well, maybe not Ava, Myla, Maya and Corbyn. Because I want them to come with me.

Me: And where would you go?

Mia: First, we'd go into [my brother] Ryan's nursery and rescue him.

Me: Haha. Nice of you to think of him.

Mia: Then I would give all my friends magical powers too.

Me: Aw that's kind of you. What would it be like if everyone had magical powers?

Mia: I guess it would be fun. Although Ryan is not allowed.

Me: Why not?

Mia: He is too young.

Me: At what age should you be allowed magical powers?

Mia: From 5 years old.

Me: And why is that?

Mia: Because you don't know how to say "Abracadabra" before that.

Reacting to a news story on TV

Mia: Can children go to prison?

Me: Normally no. Some grown-ups do though.

Mia: Why?

Me: If they've been naughty...

Mia: ...someone will call the police and take them away.

Me: Right. But how do you know if they are really guilty?

Mia: Because the person calling will tell them.

Me: But what if they're not telling the truth?

Mia: What. Grown-ups don't lie.

Me: Unfortunately sometimes some people do. Have you ever lied?

Putting things in order

Mia: Daddy, Mummy, Mia, Ryan.

Me: What's that?

Mia: How tall our family is. In order.

Me: Ah OK, I see. Very good. What's the order of our hair length?

Mia: Erm...Mia, Mummy, Ryan, Daddy.

[Thinking how to stretch the brain; for context, our family is Indian in origin so we all have brown skin]

Me: Cool. And what about skin colour?

Mia: Well, Daddy, you are very dark. And we are all light.

Me: Haha, why is that?

Mia: Because you eat too many dark chocolates.

Me: Guilty as charged.

Talking about magic wands

Me: Should everyone have magic wands?

Mia: No.

Me: Why is that?

Mia: Because then everyone would turn everyone else into a frog.

Me: Haha. Is that the only thing you can do with a wand?

Mia: I'm not sure.

[I hand her a pen.]

Me: Imagine this was your magic wand. What would you do with it?

Mia: I would wave it around to open the door for me, then it would get me ready, then it would give me breakfast, then...

Me: Ah OK so it would do everything for you?

Mia: Yes and mummy and daddy wouldn't know I had a magic wand because it is invisible.

Me: Is it important that it is invisible?

Mia: Yes, because then I can get it to do homework for me also and no one would know.

Talking about magic wands - again.

Mia: I wish I had a magic wand.

Me: What would you do with it?

Mia: Make the house rainbow coloured and also wave it at night to make the morning come quicker.

Me: Haha, very good. If mummy had a magic wand what do you think she would do with it?

Mia: Wave it to clean up the kitchen by itself so she can play with us more.

Me: I'm sure she would love that. And what about your little brother Ryan?

Mia: Well, he would probably just drop it on the floor because he likes making a mess.

The best age to have these conversations

You might have noticed these conversation examples feature children who are at least six years old.

Younger than this their vocabulary is not normally developed enough to have the type of conversations we have seen so far. Of course your children might be different and if they are particularly articulate I encourage you to give it a go.

So six years old might be the 'minimum' age, but is there a 'maximum' age?

Probably not.

Parents always tell me the questions I pose are suitable for adults as well. And they are right of course.

Human learning doesn't stop at a specific age, even more so when learning life skills like creativity, communication and critical thinking.

So these questions should be relevant to all ages.

Having said that, parents do report having these sorts of coaching conversations with pre-teens and teenagers can be tricky.

Once kids turn 12 years old many have just transitioned from a small primary school to a big secondary school. It's a generalisation but they may have now got a mobile phone and so the world of social media is beckoning. Maybe they are hitting puberty and adolescence issues are also kicking in.

Again, every child is different but on the whole parents tell me before kids turn 12 is the best time to start working these conversations into a routine. At a younger 'sweeter' age they are more likely to want to listen, engage and be curious about what you have to say.

This is not to say this all evaporates overnight when they turn 12 years old of course – and again every child is different and you know yours best.

But it's just one of the many good reasons to have lots of 'Little Big' conversations as soon as you can. It could help to keep your children more connected to you as they grow up and as they get into their teenage years.

Not to mention the wonderful brain-changing work a good conversation can do of course. That's the focus of the next chapter.

CHAPTER 7

What is the evidence this will actually work?

*"Follow the evidence wherever it leads,
and question everything."*

Neil de Grasse Tyson

You can skip this chapter if you want.

If you are totally sold on the value and benefits of talking more to your kids in the open-ended and thought-provoking way I am championing, then you won't need to see the proof it works.

Of course, you might still be curious to see which creditable organisations advocate this and the research studies show the power of doing this at home with our kids.

If so, do read on.

The 30 million word gap

Let's start with a famous one.

In 2003, researchers from the University of Kansas, Hart and Risley, wrote a paper called The Early Catastrophe. They found in a 'professional' family that talks to one another compared with a family on 'welfare' that also talk to one another, children will experience over 30 million more words at home by their fourth birthday.[1] Perhaps not surprising, but crucially follow-up studies showed these differences in language and interactions had lasting effects on the children's performances later in life.

Since then there has been a bit of back and forth on this study (typical of most research that gains widespread traction). To help you make up your mind I'm also including links here to a critical review of it[2], a defence of it[3] and a fairly balanced view[4] of it.

Broadly summarising though - the critics say the sample sizes are a bit small, but the supporters say the exact number shouldn't matter, just that there is a sizeable and observable difference and we should keep the focus on healthy dialogue with young children at home.

I am definitely in the latter camp.

More recently the research has become more nuanced also, with a recognition it is not just the quantity of words but the quality of the dialogue that matters.

Child development researcher Rowe found in 2012 the 'quality' of talk was correlated with later language development in children - even when accounting for socio-economic differences. The way to do this, the research demonstrated, is to "ask challenging questions and incorporate a diverse and sophisticated vocabulary."[5]

And in 2018 a study in Psychological Science showed how conversation lights up the brain. Amazingly it found a connection between the words a child hears at home and the growth of their neural processing capacities. Better quality talk at home, it seems, wires our kids' brains differently.[6]

Finally, a Harvard review titled The Brain Changing Power of Conversation further highlights the connection of the home language environment to a child's cognitive development, i.e. the impact parents can have by just talking with their kids.

The conversational turns and the back and forth is vitally important: "Don't just talk to your child; talk with your child. The interaction, more than the number of words a child hears, creates measurable changes in the brain and sets the stage for strong literacy skills in school."[7]

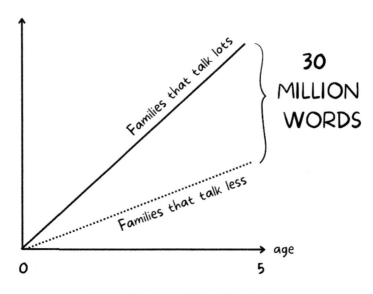

Fig 8: The 30 Million Word Gap

Clear from Covid

There's a good chance you are reading this not long after the Covid-19 pandemic. This was a monumental time for all of us with massive upheaval for parents and children. Many schools largely closed during lockdown and children spent lots of time at home with their parents.

There have been some fascinating insights coming out from all of this.

One study looked at over 500 families with children at nursery and found their social, emotional and cognitive outcomes were all improved when their parents engaged in 'enriching activities' during lockdown.[8]

This might have been reading, arts, gardening, cooking and of course having conversations. There was more growth observed in children's vocabularies and cognitive skills during this time in the children who were offered enriching activities versus those that were not.[8]

A clear argument, I think, for the power of parents.

The structure of the activities is also important

Previous research by del Bono et al in 2016 found mothers who engaged in 'structured activities' with their children (e.g. reading, playing sport, doing arts and crafts) had an association with better primary school grades and cognitive skills as opposed to engagement in 'unstructured activities' (e.g. watching the television or playing on a computer).[9]

In other words - spending time with our kids is of course very important, but if we want maximum bang for buck we should consider doing something with a bit of structure.

Like a guided conversation perhaps?

Some schools do it too

When I first had the idea about asking kids questions, I started talking to some teachers and parents about it. One such person was Hital – a family friend, and teacher at a primary school in the UK.

I explained my idea: lots of open-ended questions for kids with no right answer, to promote discussion and thought.

"Sounds exactly like Philosophy for Children," said Hital.

"What's that?" I asked.

"Philosophy for Children. They do it in some schools as a timetabled activity. Kids in class discuss life's big questions. You should check it out."

So I did. And I loved what I saw.

What is Philosophy for Children?

Philosophy for Children, or P4C as it is affectionately known by advocates, is an inquiry-based learning approach adopted by many schools.[10]

The idea is that children come up with questions they want to talk about, often after watching or reading a stimulus. For example after reading 'The Three Little Pigs' children might want to explore the topic of 'strength' and discuss a question like *Do you always need to be strong?* Or after watching a YouTube clip of a space rocket launch children might decide to explore the theme of 'exploration' and dig into a question like *Will we ever stop discovering things?*

The skills developed typically include the 4Cs of thinking: critical, creative, caring and collaborative thinking.

The teacher is the facilitator, asking questions and bringing different children into the discussions. Children tend to love these sessions as there is no right answer, their opinions matter and they get to talk lots in class.

Sapere is the UK's national charity for Philosophy for Children. On their website they write: "P4C is also a place for play. Young children ask questions about ideas that are alive for them, such as magic, friendship and play. When they do, they reveal to adults, and to themselves, their interests and inner lives. Children enjoy philosophy as a special space to experiment with ideas, express themselves and be challenged."[11]

You can see the similarity to what I am writing about in this book. In some ways all I am doing is urging the extension of P4C from mainstream schools into the home environment.

Sometimes people question whether children are mature enough to be philosophers. Nowadays we tend to think of philosophers as deep thinkers with PhDs postulating existential musings, whereas the original form of Philosophy was merely asking simple, curious questions (the Socratic approach).

Jana Mohr Lone is a champion of P4C and in her book The Philosophical Child she writes:

"During those early years, children are wide open to the philosophical mysteries that pervade human life, often lying awake at night thinking about such issues as whether God exists, why the world has the colours it does, what the nature of time might be, whether dreams are real, why we die and what is the meaning of life. Almost as soon as they can formulate them, children start asking what we would call 'big questions.' Brimming with curiosity about aspects of the world that most adults take for granted, children demonstrate a natural human capacity to explore the most basic elements of human life and society."[12]

Expert Insights:
Nick Chandley - Former Primary School Teacher and Director at DialogueWorks[13]

When I'm working in schools, I often meet the frustration from teachers that children don't seem to ask very 'philosophical' questions.

My response to this is that all questions have philosophical potential, which is only unlocked through careful listening and sensitive probing. For example, I was once faced with this question, asked by a class of 9/10 year-olds in Norfolk, UK.

I had just shown them a short video of an elephant painting a picture of an elephant and they asked *How much do these paintings sell for?*

This, on the face of it, was a request for a factual response, and as I knew the answer, I told the children – between £400 - £4,000. This could have been the end of the conversation, but I then asked, *But why did you ask that question?*

The children replied with, "Because we wanted to find out if the paintings were being sold for lots of money". Being a particularly persistent (or annoying) person, I then asked, *Why did you want to know that?*

The response this time was if the paintings were sold for lots of money, as indeed they were, who gets the money? I then asked, *Why do you want to know who gets the money?*

They said they wanted to know because it would be unfair for the keepers to get the money when the elephants created the art.

So, here is the philosophical door opening. Only a little at the moment, but a little is all you need. I can now follow this up with a whole range of 'philosophical' questions, such as:

How do we decide how much a piece of art is worth?

Should humans profit from animals?

What counts as 'exploitation'?

...and so on. But what is important here is this, ultimately, philosophical discussion arose from a question asked by the children, so they felt ownership of the process. This, for me, is incredibly important, because if we were to dismiss children's questions as lower-quality ones and then replace them with our own, then we reinforce the notion that we, as adults, are the 'clever' ones, asking all the good questions.

At the end of this session with the children in Norfolk, I could confidently say to the children their question stimulated a wonderful discussion.

So – be annoying and add *But why did you ask that question?* to your armoury.

Proof that P4C works

As you can expect with any teaching methodology, the use of Philosophy for Children is underpinned by evidence-based research. It has clearly shown that children who do P4C - having a mindset of questioning, dialogue and reflection - outperform other children in maths, literacy and cognitive reasoning. In addition it has been shown to have positive effects on wellbeing and teamwork. Best of all, Philosophy for Children seems to have an amplified positive effect on disadvantaged children.

The Education Endowment Foundation in the UK is the de facto group that gauges the strength of different education interventions in terms of progress of academic attainment, i.e. what helps kids learn more and quicker?

In 2015 they found:[14]

- All P4C students had two months of additional progress in reading and maths.
- Disadvantaged students had four months of progress in reading and three months in maths.
- Both teachers and pupils said they were feeling more confident, patient and reported higher self-esteem.

A follow up study by the Education Endowment Foundation in 2021 found:[15]

- 96% of teachers felt P4C helped pupils to respect others' opinions.
- 91% of teachers felt P4C improved pupils' ability to question and reason.

- 93% of teachers felt P4C improved pupils' ability to express views clearly.

Finally, the Nuffield Foundation in the UK ran a study to explore the non-cognitive impacts of P4C. In 2017 they found:[16]

- P4C students felt they were better at communication skills, teamwork and resilience.
- This effect was more pronounced with those from disadvantaged families.

The Oracy movement

What are the most important subjects at mainstream schools? Which are considered the most fundamental, get the most teaching time and the highest exam focus?

If you thought of maths and English, then you're right. Numeracy and literacy have been a mainstay of traditional education for hundreds of years, and understandably so.

But let's not forget about the poor forgotten cousin of Oracy.[17] This is the ability to speak and listen well which, last time I checked, is also pretty fundamental to function in society.

Given we humans are all social creatures and do our best work in large groups, it seems odd that most traditional education systems do not prioritise communication skills in this way.

Voice 21 is a champion of Oracy in the UK.[18] They have been doing an incredible job since they were founded in 2014 to thrust speaking and listening skills into the limelight, working with government, schools and teachers to devote more class time to the development of these precious skills.

They highlight several clear advantages of Oracy on their website:

1. Oracy improves academic outcomes, developing learners who can think critically, reason together and have the vocabulary to express their knowledge and understanding.
2. Oracy fosters wellbeing and confidence, empowering students to build successful relationships and realise their voice has value.
3. Oracy equips students to thrive in democratic and civic life, citizenship requires us to express our views and listen kindly and critically.
4. Oracy promotes social equity, leading to a fairer society where everyone, regardless of background, finds their voice for success in school and life.
5. Oracy increases engagement in learning.

Backed by the University of Cambridge

Neil Mercer, a Cambridge Professor of Education, has done lots of work on Exploratory Talk and Dialogic Teaching.

He writes on his website that "Spoken language enables us to do much more than share information - it enables us to think together".[19]

I couldn't agree more. Talking and thinking are so interwoven, which is why I love being able to bring the two together.

A paper Neil co-authored cites a US study that says, "The amount and quality of the dialogue children experience at home in the preschool years correlated strongly with their eventual academic attainment".[20]

I was lucky enough to work with Neil in the development of the KidCoachApp. One area he was able to advise us on rather well was how to encourage conversational turns. This simply means helping dialogue go back and forth (a bit like playing verbal tennis), exactly what the Harvard review highlights as being so important.

It's a good one to bear in mind as you engage in more conversations with your child. What can you say or do to keep the tennis rally going?

Funnily enough, this was exactly what one of my previous bosses said to me. Her name is Holly and she is hands down the most sociable, chatty and people-oriented business leader I have ever had the good fortune to work with. She told me once how, when she was growing up, her father used to train her and her siblings in having verbal tennis rallies with people they would meet at parties.

I have no doubt Holly's upbringing in this Oracy-rich environment was a leading contributor to her being a fantastic communicator in the workplace today.

PART C: HOW?

CHAPTER 8

How can I engage my kids and hold their interest?

"Adults are only kids grown up, anyway."

Walt Disney

It's the weekend. You find yourself with five minutes with the kids. This book has inspired you to try asking more quirky questions and so you give one a go.

And then you hit a brick wall.

It could be that your child repeatedly says, "I don't know." Or maybe they give a one-word response and then run off to play with their Nintendo Switch, uninterested in carrying on the conversation.

If that does happen to you then don't worry. It's extremely common.

In this chapter, I'll share some practical tips you can use to start better conversations, as well as tips to keep them going.

Lean into their interests

Kids love talking about things they are into. If you start off with a topic they are passionate about then you are stacking the deck in your favour.

Let's use the example of football.

I talked with 7-year-old Ryan recently who was a big football fan. He supports Liverpool FC, in the UK, which is managed by Jurgen Klopp. At the time of writing they are playing quite well.

I was able to use this single topic of football to have a variety of conversations that built skills from leadership to critical thinking, and from communication to philosophy.

How would you describe the game of football to an alien? (Communication)

Ryan jumped straight in and started talking about formations and tactics and team names. This is classic behaviour with kids, particularly if it's a topic they get excited by.

Of course, it would make zero sense to an alien who has no clue what football is, so this was a good coaching moment to help him to take a beginner's perspective and work on explaining something he knows well but as simply as possible.

To coach him in orientating his listener I used prompts such as *How do you win? What are the three most important rules? Why do people like it?*

Is VAR a good thing? (Critical Thinking)

VAR stands for Video Assistant Referees. Introduced in 2019, they allow controversial decisions to be replayed and a referee in a digital room somewhere to help make the right decision retrospectively.

There have been ups and downs to this and this question got Ryan thinking from different perspectives. He thought it helped the referees to make the right decision, but admits it does slow down the game. I used reflective prompts such as *What do the referees think of VAR? Is it worth the technology cost? How will the VAR introduction be seen in 20 years?*

What makes Jurgen Klopp a good leader? (Leadership)

The Liverpool manager has been very successful with his own style. His key attribute is personality. Klopp is very much a people person and manages to motivate his team very effectively. I got Ryan talking and thinking about this by asking prompts such as *How is Klopp different to other managers? What's an example of how he motivated the team? What do you think other managers say about him?*

Should footballers get paid so much? (Philosophy)

The average Liverpool football player gets paid millions of pounds a year, which is rather a lot. How much they really ought to be paid is very subjective, but I wanted Ryan to form a view and explain why he thinks that. His initial response was "Yes, they should be paid this money," after which I tested his resolve by asking prompting questions such as *How much money do doctors, nurses and teachers get in comparison? What else could be done with that money? Is it the fault of footballers that they are paid so much?*

More questions on things your kids are into

If your child is not into football or sports you may have glazed over that last bit. Don't worry. In Appendix III I give you lots more examples of questions you can use if your kids are into things like books (e.g. Harry Potter), video games (e.g. Fortnite), hobbies (e.g. art) and much more.

Expert Insights:
Dr Kate Cross - Senior Educational and Child Psychologist

Children love spending time with their parents. Time and time again, research has shown the more parents engage in daily conversations with their children, the more rapidly children's vocabularies and confidence grows. However, sometimes it can be challenging to engage children in meaningful conversations, especially when parents are competing with devices/technology to gain attention. After school, many children are tired and don't want 'more work' to do. Therefore, it is important to make conversations more fun, interactive and perhaps linked to a topic of interest for a child.

The use of an interactive prop can be fun and exciting for children. They can help keep children engaged, as well as make the conversation topic more concrete, as opposed to abstract. For example, if asking *What are 10 different things you could do with a cup?* a child is likely to think of more ideas with a physical cup present. It may not be natural to use a prop for all questions or conversations but they can be a useful tool to gently ease children into back and forth conversation.

Children like to talk about themselves so reflecting questions back to them is another way to engage them further in conversations. For example when asking *What is gratefulness?* a parent could ask their child if there is anything/anybody they are grateful for and why. A parent could also ask prompting questions like *What does feeling grateful feel like in your body?* or *When do you feel most grateful?* Asking questions that include children's thoughts, feelings and experiences are likely to generate more engagement and longer conversations.

Finding the time to have more engaging conversations can be a challenge for most busy families. Often when parents want to talk, children don't and vice versa. The best time for conversations are when everyone is relaxed and not under time pressure. Doing something together, whether it be eating dinner, going for a walk or colouring and drawing jointly, can lead to more engaging conversations, as children are relaxed when the 'pressure' to have a conversation is removed. The car can be a great place to have conversations with children as they don't have to make eye contact, which can make some children uncomfortable.

Use props

Children love to play with and touch things. The tactile feeling of turning an object around in your hand also seems to trigger thoughts that would not have come otherwise. Speaking to Dr

Kate Cross, an educational and child psychologist I work with, she also told me how props can engage an otherwise reluctant child and get a conversation going.

Below are some questions and suggestions based on props you would easily find at home.

- Cup: *What are 10 things we could do with a cup?* (Creativity)
- Toy car: *How would you describe a car to an alien?* (Communication)
- 5 x £20 Monopoly notes: *How would you go and make £100 next month?* (Critical Thinking)
- Family iPad: *How can you estimate the number of iPads in the UK?* (Analytics)
- Alarm clock: *Should children be allowed to set their own bedtime?* (Debating)
- Colouring pencils: *What would you call a new colour that you invented?* (Creativity)
- Yourself: *Why do we have two ears and one mouth?* (Leadership)

By the way, the first one can be done with any object in the house. It is a very helpful hack to build creativity in a quick and fun way. Just grab any object you see in the house, give it to your child and ask them *What are 10 things you can do with this X?*

Just like doing press-ups, the first few will be easy but then it gets harder. This is when the creativity muscle is being built the most, so keep going.

Say you are in the kitchen and you grab an apple. You can ask *What are 10 things you can do with an apple?*

"Eat it" is the obvious one. But what else? How about making apple pie, or playing catch, or learning about gravity etc? Can you get to 10?

Pass the mic

When you are having a conversation as a family do you sometimes end up talking over one another?

I experienced this a lot with my two kids. I'm always so proud when my eldest wants to talk, but sometimes it's difficult for my younger child to get a word in, or vice versa.

So we got a big spoon from the kitchen and pretended it was a microphone. The person talking got to use it and then passed it on when they were done. This ensured everyone's voice was heard and everyone had their moment in the limelight.

To be honest, it helps keep me in check too. Sometimes we parents can be guilty of talking too much, being so eager to share our years of wisdom. Passing the 'mic' has helped me keep my speeches short.

Use natural stimuli around you

One effortless way of having skill-building conversations is to use the natural stimuli around you. You might be at home, walking into town or eating at a restaurant. This makes the conversations run naturally and won't feel like learning at all.

Consider some of these locations.

At home

- *This sofa seems fine, but how could we make it better?* (Critical Thinking)
- *We have enough food to eat. But is it OK that some people in other countries do not?* (Philosophy)
- *Lots of people watch TV. What message would you put on it if you could?* (Leadership)
- *What are 10 different things you could do with this pen?* (Creativity)

Walking in town

- *How do we get home from here?* (Communication)
- *How do you think that person is feeling?* (Empathy)
- *What animal does that cloud look like?* (Creativity)
- *What shop could you open here and what could it sell?* (Critical Thinking)

Eating at a restaurant

- *How could you rename this restaurant?* (Creativity)
- *What type of restaurant makes the most money and why?* (Critical Thinking)
- *Is having lots of choices a good thing?* (Philosophy)
- *Can you place our order for us?* (Confidence)

If you struggle to think of these sorts of questions on the spot then don't worry. Practice makes perfect. The more you challenge yourself to think of questions it will wire your brain to look for similar sorts of questions in more natural settings.

Or there is my handy app you are welcome to try.

Ask Why (a lot)

It's time to turn the tables.

Remember when your child was quite young and they would ask *Why?* all the time? Well, now it's your turn. This simple three-letter word is fantastic at helping children think more critically and solve problems. Other variants are *Why do you want to do that? Why do you think that? Why, what happened?*

Take this example I saw on the internet.[1] A dad had asked his son Billy to mow the lawn, but when he came home it had not been done.

Dad: Why did the lawn not get mowed?

Billy: Because the mower broke.

Dad: Why did the mower break?

[Billy investigates]

Billy: The bearing has burned out.

Dad: Why did the bearing burn out?

[Billy investigates more]

Billy: I think it wasn't oiled properly.

Dad: Why had it not been oiled properly?

Billy: Looks like the oil line was plugged.

Dad: Why was the oil line plugged?

Billy: Because we haven't been maintaining the lawnmower regularly.

The dad is helping Billy be more investigative. In this example it is not about pointing the finger or telling Billy off. Rather, it is using the power of why to help Billy figure out what was the root cause of the problem and how they can fix this together.

Start easy, then get harder

When we want our children to think about difficult things, it's a good idea to start with an easier smaller question and then make it harder as we go along. Let's take the previous example of: *What are 10 different things you can do with a cup?*

Parent: What are 10 different things you can do with a cup?

Child: Erm, you can drink from it.....not sure what else.

Parent: If the cup was upside down it could be a drum. What else could you do with it upside down?

Child: Ah, you could stack them to make towers....you could use them as pins and play ten pin bowling...

Parent: Great stuff, anything else?

Child: Erm, not sure...?

Parent: OK, well what if we made the cup really big. Like REALLY big. The size of a house.

Child: That's a big cup. Maybe it could be like a swimming pool then? Or a climbing frame like in a playground.

Parent: Haha, very creative, well done.

Notice how the first prompt about playing the drums upside down was easier since it was a statement that turned into a question. The second prompt about the cup being really big was more open-ended and harder.

This is called 'scaffolding'. It is a teaching term which means to "move students progressively toward stronger understanding and, ultimately, greater independence in the learning process."[2]

As parents, we don't need to get too technical about it, but it's good to know a simple trick like this can help us to help our kids figure stuff out.

All the prompts we have in the KidCoachApp are scaffolded like this, so you can just ask the question and enjoy the conversation.

Adopt different (animal) attitudes

When talking with my kids I sometimes find it helpful to adopt a certain mood or attitude. It helps me to channel the best sorts of questions. In particular I like to think of animals like bees, rhinos, eagles and ants:

- Bees are curious – investigating, probing, searching.
- Rhinos are challenging– poking holes, pushing back, defying.

- Eagles are conceptual – elevating, thinking higher, imagining.
- Ants are collaborative – using others, open-minded, working together.

When talking with our kids we can adopt any of these different 'animal' attitudes.

Each has their time and place and will also depend on your particular child (you might not want to be a challenging rhino lots with a highly sensitive child).

Let's use the starter example of *Should everyone give money to charity?*

Here are some prompting questions you can ask:

- Curious bee: *What are your thoughts on this? How did you make up your mind? How do you feel about your answer?*
- Challenging rhino: *Why would some people not agree with that? In what situation is that not true? Can you convince me otherwise?*
- Conceptual eagle: *Why is this an important question? What do we mean by charity? How have people's attitudes to this changed over the years?*
- Collaborative ants: *What would your friends say to this? Who else can we ask for their view? What more information would help us decide?*

This might be a good approach for grown-up discussions as well by the way. Maybe you want to be the collaborative ant with your work colleague but a challenging rhino when dealing with a salesperson.

Modelling

Life imitates art and kids imitate big people. If we are trying to coach children in a certain way we would do well to model (show them) what we mean.

Perhaps the next time your child asks you a quirky question of their own, you could show them how you don't know the answer but are eager and curious to think about it?

In the past few years my kids have asked me all sorts. Maybe you have got some of these wonderful questions as well:

- *Why is the sky blue?*
- *Why is the Moon following me?*
- *Why do grown ups not go to school?*
- *Do babies know they are babies?*
- *What is a dream?*

Each time I've tried to stifle my instinctive "I don't know" response and instead say something like:

- *Great question. What do you think?*
- *I'm not sure but let's find out*
- *Shall we Google search it?*
- *Who can we ask to help us figure it out?*
- *I think that...*

Modelling is an incredibly powerful parenting tool. Not just with ways to talk and think, but more generally ways to be as a human being.

When your kids are all grown up, wouldn't it be wonderful if they approached any tricky situation with a musing such as *What would mum do?* or *What would dad do?*

Make a provocative statement

This is an approach championed by Lyn Dawes, Education Consultant at the University of Cambridge. She likes to create 'provocative statements' which are slightly controversial ideas, phrased in ways to get kids talking. She calls them Talking Points and has written a book about their use in the classroom.[3]

They are a change from asking questions, and because they have no right or wrong answer, provide the chance to explore a range of views just by talking around them.

Let's revisit our example from before: *Should everyone give money to charity?* Here are some Talking Points you could use to stoke the conversational flames. Thanks to Lyn for sharing these with me:

- *If everybody worked hard, we would not need charities.*
- *Charities waste money.*
- *There should just be one charity that would help everyone.*
- *Charities that help people are more important than charities that help animals.*
- *Rich people should donate more money to charity.*

- *Charities make people feel bad to get them to donate.*

Making one of these statements does not mean you have to believe it. It's just a way of activating a child's curiosity in ways that they can't help but respond.

You can take this idea and apply it to all sorts of situations, not just chats about charities. What about these simple statements which help your child engage with complex ideas.

Again courtesy of Lyn:

- Life *is fun.*
- *Today is better than yesterday.*
- *If we try hard we can always get what we want.*
- *People stop learning when they stop being kids.*
- *No two people are the same.*
- *I always like my friends.*
- *Needing something and wanting something are the same.*
- *People only cry when they are feeling sorry for themselves.*

I love this approach and find it works well with my kids when my quirky questions aren't landing for some reason. It seems harder to ignore a provocative statement than it does a searching question, and the kids can't help but say something.

What provocative statements can you come up with today? Try it out with your kids.

Be positive with praise

Children can get scared of getting answers wrong. Possibly this is due to rigid school systems and modern assessment techniques only working when a response is either right or wrong.

At home, even when we parents are deliberately asking questions with no right answer to explore all the shades of grey, children can sometimes need some encouragement to engage in this new breed of question.

In these situations, we can slow down and just make some simple encouraging utterances.

The following list works well in almost every situation. I really recommend sprinkling them into your conversations with kids, whatever you are doing:

- *Keep going.*
- *Hmm, interesting.*
- *You are getting really good at these.*
- *Wow, you have so many thoughts here.*
- *I love that word you used.*
- *Amazing listening. I liked how you built on what I just said.*
- *Great point. I hadn't thought of that.*

This is in line with Carol Dweck's work on praise and growth mindset.[4] She often talks about the benefits of praising children's efforts and engagement over the outcomes and results. In the context of these conversations we can be praising the attempt at talking before we judge the quality of thinking.

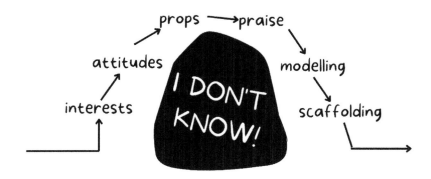

Fig 9: Getting Around "I don't Know"

Silence is OK

I'm giving you lots of prompting question options here, but there are times when it's best just to say nothing at all.

When there is a void, we parents often feel the urge to fill it with chatter. But children are more comfortable with silence than adults are. We might think our child is pausing because they haven't understood, which makes us want to help or clarify. Sometimes however they are just processing the information and considering their reply, so let's give them the time and space to do so. Just count to five in your head before you jump in.

As one parent said to me after I had held a coaching session with her daughter for our podcast: "It was absolutely genius the way you mixed taking time to listen to what she had to say and bringing the answers out of her".

I'm no genius (let me assure you of that). We can all make this approach work.

CHAPTER 9

How can we find more family time to have these conversations?

"The bad news is time flies. The good news is that you're the pilot."

Michael Altshuler - Global Speaker and Success Coach

We have looked at how to engage children and addressed any hesitancy kids might have about these conversations. But what about with us parents and caregivers?

I understand this new way of talking could feel like a big change. The key word here is 'feel' because, in reality, there isn't much change.

We are still using the same time we have, the same tools we have and the same people are involved. But still, it might feel unusual to begin with.

So this chapter is all about how to make this easy and natural in your lives, so it slots into the rhythm and routine of your family unit.

How can I find the time to do this?

This is one of the questions I get asked most frequently. And the answer I give sometimes sounds too simple, but it's true.

Just use the time you already spend with your kids.

As I've mentioned before, kids who go to school only spend about 20% of their time there. That means a whopping 80% is spent outside of school, primarily at home with parents.

It might be on the school run, walking down to the shops, waiting in line somewhere, going out for dinner or putting them to bed. In each of these places we are together and, while we may not have fancy gadgets or games with us, we do have the one thing we truly need - our voices. Unless it's at the dentist, there aren't many situations where we can't get into some great conversations with our kids.

Now I know life is hectic and the time you do have with your kids is super busy. Of course, you already talk a lot to your kids during this time. It's just I suspect some of those conversations could be made less transactional and more meaningful.

Make it a healthy habit

Arguably one of the most important pieces of advice I can give you on how to introduce conversations like this with your kids is how to make it a regular feature in your routine.

When you want to lose weight you go on a new diet. When you want to get more energy you go on an exercise regime. When you want to save money you browse in the discount aisle of the supermarket. After a few weeks, each of these things becomes a new healthy habit in your life.

It's the same with having better conversations with kids. Here are some helpful tips, many from parents I work with:

- State your intentions: make it clear why you are doing this. Maybe it was to connect more with your kids, to improve their confidence, or to get them talking more? Whatever it was - write it down.
- Schedule the time: if it's not in the calendar then it won't get done. One mum told me she has a regular calendar entry for when the kids are back from school, called 'snack and chat.'
- Make it visible: if you want to use a specific app more, one neat trick is to move the app icon to your home screen where you will regularly see it. One mum sent me a screenshot of her phone, where the KidCoachApp icon was sandwiched between Facebook and Google. What a simple yet effective idea.
- Stack the habit: this is when you combine one new habit with one old habit, to help the new one stick. One dad told me he does 20 press-ups each time he flicks on the kettle. Can you pick one moment in the day where you are doing something routine with the kids, like driving them home from school, and decide to have a 'Little Big' conversation with them then?
- Do it together: conversations work well as a family, so try to include other people where possible, e.g. your partner, grandparents, an older child etc. If one is not available then you could summarise the conversation later on as a way of sharing a memorable experience.

- Make a commitment: when you make a financial commitment to something you are more likely to use it. One friend of mine bought a Peloton bike for £2,000 just to make sure she used it to get fit. And it worked.

Start with your beliefs

One more important point on this, comes from the book Atomic Habits by James Clear.[1] The author refers to your self-beliefs as being the key to making a new healthy habit: "Behind every system of actions is a system of beliefs. It is hard to change your habits if you never change your underlying beliefs."

This means if you want to adopt the KidCoach approach, then you need to believe in your heart the following.

Try saying these out loud to yourself now:

- "I am my child's best coach."
- "I can prepare my child for the future."
- "I know how to ask really good questions."
- "It doesn't matter if I don't know the answer."
- "My child loves to talk with me."

How did that feel?

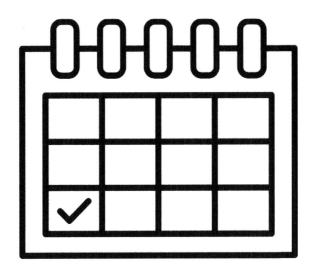

Fig 10: Making the Habit

Expert Insights:
Anita Cleare - parenting expert and author of The Work/Parent Switch[2]

Modern parents are incredibly busy. When it comes to parenting, it can feel like everything matters.

We judge ourselves as parents on every front – the grades our kids achieve at school, the clubs they attend, their kindness, their behaviour, their eating habits and table manners. It's easy to get side tracked and approach parenting as a huge 'To Do' list that must be squeezed into the bits of time left over when work is done.

However, if you truly want to engage in more meaningful conversations with your kids, you need to approach parenting as a relationship, not as a list of tasks to be completed. You need to learn to manage your mindset, turn off your 'to do' list efficiency thinking and dial up your curiosity.

Having good transition rituals between work and parenting can really help. The next time you finish work and are about to see your children, pause for two minutes. Close your eyes and imagine their faces in as much detail as you can. Once you can see them in your mind's eye, smile. Allow the positive feelings to sweep through you and just breathe. You might use a happy memory to help with this, or a photo of your child. You might find it useful to recite a personal phrase such as "Now, I am mum."

Taking a minute to reset your mindset into parent mode makes it much more likely you will approach your children in the present moment rather than always rushing three steps ahead. You'll be more likely to notice when the opportunity arises for a great conversation and be truly invested in it, curious and playful.

And the best news is when we learn to step into a more curious, present-focused mode with our kids, we also reap the benefits in terms of increased wellbeing, decreased stress and that precious feeling of really getting something right as a parent.

Where to have these conversations

I've been working with thousands of parents now and so I asked them - where do you have the best conversations with your kids and why?

Here is what they said:

- The car: kids can't go anywhere so they have to talk to you. There is so much opportunity for you to have conversations about where you are going or what you see during the drive. Sitting side by side also takes the pressure off chatting and kids seem to respond well in this kind of set-up.

- The dinner table: perhaps the ultimate family time location, this is a safe space for more serious topics, as well as more light-hearted catch ups. By sitting at the table together, there is the potential to bond over the food and take the time to be thoughtful with remarks.

- The school run: this 5-10 minute walk is fast but can be made fun with quirky questions. For some parents it is nice one-on-one time with an individual child. On the way back from school it makes for a much better alternative to the usual *How was school today?*

- In bed: winding down at the end of the day, many children open up and share what's on their mind. It is a good time to talk about mental health and feelings as you lie down and physically get on the same level as your child.

- Waiting for something: it feels like we are always in a queue for something nowadays. Remember to use the environment around you, say at a restaurant or shop or post office, asking questions about food or money or jobs.

- Relaxing on the sofa: this is the only place listed where there is no multitasking going on. Some parents like to carve out some specific KidCoach time where they are purposefully setting aside time for a quick chat.

Two things we always do in the car

If your family is anything like ours I bet you are in the car a lot. Going to the supermarket, visiting relatives or being the chauffeur for the weekend activities - we all seem to rack up quite a few minutes in the car with the kids.

Over the years we've managed to build up a couple of awesome habits for any car journey like this.

The first is actually nothing to do with talking. It's about healthy eating and I mention this just to illustrate how anyone can build new habits. We take five minutes before we leave to cut some vegetable sticks like peppers, carrots and cucumbers for the kids. They happily munch away on these and have now come to associate driving with veggie sticks. (We have my wife to thank for all of this. She is a health coach at 'Emma's Healthy Habits' if you are at all interested.)

The second habit is more conversational. We've got into the habit of playing talking games like 'I Went To The Supermarket', 'I Spy', 'Yes And' etc. Again the kids have come to associate this with driving and actively ask to play each time.

Our favourite is the 'Connecting' game. This is a verbal association game where you take turns going around the car saying a single word. Each word must somehow be connected to the word before.

Example: "tree", "leaf", "green", "paint", "wall", "clock", ."hands" We go as fast as you can and to make it harder we sometimes put in a rule where you have to cycle through letters in the alphabet e.g. "apple", "bowl", "cup", "drink", "eat" etc.

It's also good for a few giggles. There have been a few times when our youngest has just said the word "toilet", completely unconnected to the previous word, just for a laugh.

But it's so new to me

It might feel a bit strange starting out. Say your child is 10 years old and you haven't engaged with them in this way before. Of course, you have spoken and had lots of quality time with your kid. But you haven't ever really asked them these kinds of questions before or tried to have long conversations like this with them. You may feel a bit silly or uncertain.

It's normal. Don't worry.

Trying anything for the first time is a bit strange but that's okay. In these moments I often remind parents of the goal. What is the point of these conversations?

In the long-term, it is to coach your kids and build some key skills you know they need to thrive. In the short-term, just see it as getting to know your kids more and creating some nice moments. So it's building skills and memories - two for one.

At the end of the day, it's only a conversation, so what's the worst that could happen? Perspective matters. All you are actually doing is having a casual chat with your kids. Stay present, grateful and engaged and you are already doing perfectly.

What if I don't feel up for it?

We all experience different moods and there might be days you don't feel like doing this. That's OK. And the same goes for your kids. No need to force conversations if one of you isn't up for it.

At the same time, it's important we don't freeze our kids out whenever we don't feel our best. Consistency is key. You don't have to show up as your best self every day, but do show up.

Be mindful of how your kids might interpret one day having tons of conversation and quality time and the next barely muttering a word to each other. It can be difficult showing up for a conversation when you don't feel your best or when time gets away from you. However a quick chat is a rapid way to get you into a better mood and stave off that guilty feeling of not spending enough time with your kids.

Here is a top tip for when you really don't feel like it.

On those odd days I just can't muster the energy to think about questions or even engage in a typical back and forth conversation with my kids, I ask a *Would you rather...?* question.

- *Would you rather be super strong or super fast?*
- *Would you rather be five years older or five years younger?*
- *Would you rather eat pizza all the time or ice cream all the time?*
- *Would you rather have hands for feet or feet for hands?*
- *Would you rather be more like mum or more like dad?"*

Would you rather questions are binary so it's easy to get started (for me and the kids). You can formulate them however you want and it pays to be silly here. Then just use the tips in this book to take the conversation deeper, with whys and other nudging prompts.

Parent Stories:
Alice - mum of six, nine and 11 year olds

My combined interest in Parenting, Technology and Education got me so interested in this conversational approach.

Working in change management, I know the importance of making something a habit. I held myself to account for choosing a question to talk through on the way to school every day, and after 28 days it was firmly embedded as a habit. The girls now ask me for the daily question.

Our favourite questions have been things like *What are 10 things to do with a cup? How would you describe a computer to an alien? What would you do if dinosaurs were alive today?*

They really love dinosaurs. My daughter wanted to have then invented dinosaurs which led to a great conversation.

Remember your why

When all else fails, remember why you are doing what you are doing.

For example: Why are you reading this book? Why have you read this far?

Probably because you are seeking some sort of change, for you and your kids? What is it?

For me, I was in search of that end of the day fist-pump feeling of a parenting job well done. I wanted to be able to high-five my wife having taken just five minutes to do something meaningful and worthwhile with the kids.

It motivated me then and still motivates me now.

When you find your why, things just seem to flow easier.

What is your why?

Summary: What happens next

"You cannot predict the outcome of human development. All you can do is like a farmer, create the conditions under which it will begin to flourish."

Sir Ken Robinson - Author, Speaker and International Education Advisor

In the introduction I promised a fast and fun book that was going to be quick and easy to read. I hope I have delivered.

In Part A we covered why you should be having these types of conversations. We showed why the world is changing so fast, why your kids will need a new set of skills to thrive in it and why the humble conversation is a fantastic way to coach them for this.

In Part B we went through lots of examples of what questions to ask and suggested some prompts to take the conversation further. We talked about asking more open-ended questions to get your kids talking and thinking, drawing on the news, images and pictures, their interests and your environment to make it all super fun and engaging.

In Part C we discussed how to engage your kids (and yourself) to make this new healthy habit stick. We shared some tips on how to build better routines and how grabbing five minutes in the car, on the school run or over the dinner table are great ways to get started.

When you put this book down and go back to your busy life with emails to answer, kids to feed and chores to do - I really hope you remember to put into practice some of what you have just read.

All too often we get inspired by something we read, but then we fail to take action. So what happens? After a few weeks the urgency fades and we forget what we learned.

Here is a simple idea that works for most people I know.

Scheduling.

Please go with me on this.

Get your phone out and create a 15 minute calendar entry to have a 'Little Big' conversation with your kids. It doesn't have to be every day, perhaps just a couple times a week to begin with. Do whatever suits your family routine - just think about where and when you can have the best chats with your kids.

Set the calendar entry to recur for three months so you keep getting prompted.

When the scheduled time arrives, use the questions in this book. Or if you want my latest and greatest questions, updated each month and with world events, then download the KidCoachApp.

Whatever you end up talking about just keep in mind you want to be having open and thoughtful discussions. It's OK if nobody knows the answer. For the first few sessions pick topics your kids will be into and then you never know, they might soon be coming to you asking for the next question.

Have you made the 'Little Big' calendar entry yet? I hope so.

I'd like to leave you with one final thought.

I think Education is the most powerful mechanism that exists to change the world quickly and for the better. And we parents are incredibly well placed to help with this.

Because if all of us Big people brought up the Little people in our lives to be wonderful human beings — who could talk well with others, think well on their feet and feel well in themselves — how amazing would the world be in just 20 years when they are all grown up?

Kavin Wadhar
Dad of 2 kids
www.kidcoach.app

Acknowledgements

This book is a culmination of years of learning from and working with some amazing people. Below I attempt to list and name everyone who has had a hand in shaping the KidCoach way of parenting. I am immensely grateful to all, and deeply apologetic to anyone I may have accidentally missed.

Education and parenting experts

- Ian Gilbert, author of Thunks, for responding to my LinkedIn message years ago and for all the advice and support shown thereafter.
- Nick Chandley, director at DialogueWorks and purveyor of great questions, for sharpening my questions and finding the philosophical angle in any topic.
- Dr Kate Cross, educational and child psychologist, for constantly reminding me to put the child at the centre of everything we do.
- Sue Atkins, parenting expert, for the overall enthusiasm and advocacy of this as a parenting approach we should all adopt.

- Neil Mercer, director of Oracy at University of Cambridge, for the inputs into developing our app and how to best supplement the work of schools.

Parent champions

- Alison Roberts, mum of nine year old, for being my first case study and always thinking about me with ideas for the app and business.
- Alice de Araujo, mum of 12, 10 and eight year olds, for sharing openly how this approach has transformed her school run and inspiring other families to do the same.
- Sonal Lakhani, mum of nine and seven year old, for being a beta tester of our questions and the app, and giving amazing feedback every step of the way.
- Sonya Modelina, mum of 12 and nine year old, for inviting me to her home in London in the early days to test out questions with her children.

App builders

- Steven Martin, for building the prototype of the KidCoachApp to such a high level of detail and consideration, that it has stood the test of time.
- Nitin Patel, for taking over the app build and helping his team iterate the app to include all sorts of features requested by parents.
- Robbert Bos, founder of the Family Five App, for his time and business mentorship to help us reach many more parents.

KidCoach team

- Dominic Walker, for helping me write so many great questions for kids, and for testing them out with several children on our podcast.
- Sophie Horan, for volunteering her time to make KidCoach Cards - our physical flashcard version of the app (available on Etsy).
- Amber Carvalho, aspiring journalist, for helping me write this book - drafting text, formatting the manuscript and editing constantly.

Editors for this book

- Sarah Lenehan, freelancing copy editor and proofreader, for doing a wonderfully thorough job going through my draft manuscript and making some fantastic suggestions.
- Elizabeth Dougherty, editor for numerous parenting books, for doing a high-level developmental edit and assuring me I was on the right lines.
- Marie Hooper, colleague and friend, for taking the time to read the manuscript in great detail, making super sensible suggestions and giving some lovely feedback on the way.
- Devila Vekria, for picking up the little things my eyes were missing.
- Suzy Davey, for reading through and making helpful suggestions throughout.

My family

- Kirit and Vandana Wadhar, my parents, for raising me to talk well, think well (and hopefully) write well also.
- Emma Wadhar, my wonderful wife, for being the constant companion to bounce ideas and frustrations off.
- Mia and Ryan, my children, for inspiring me every single day.

APPENDICES

12 skills to focus on

21st century skills, human skills, essential skills, soft skills, future skills. These skills go by many different names and different organisations have different ways of defining each. After doing a lot of research, I decided to make my own super simple framework for parents where I list 12 skills our kids will need.

I've simplified them under the categories 'Talking, Thinking and Feeling.' When I have a few minutes spare with my kids I find it helpful to think of a skill to develop first, as that narrows down the endless list of possibilities.

Talking Skills

Communication

- The human ability to communicate with each other is what leads to shared stories, inspiration and motivation. Every day there more people in the world and more connections between us all. Your child will thrive if they are brought up to communicate clearly and concisely with everyone, be it in person or over social media.

- Sample question: *How would you describe a car to an alien?*

Debating

- Debating is such a good way of developing skills in listening, communication, persuasion, critical thinking and resilience. It is no surprise amazing debaters rise to the top of their professions. I consider debating as a bit of a "super skill" and strongly recommend you have friendly debates with your child.
- Sample question: *Should children set their own bedtimes?*

Leadership

- Throughout history, humans have excelled when working in groups - and every group needs a leader. The ability to motivate, align and enable a group of people to perform optimally is what makes a leader stand out. You can nurture this in your child at a young age already by helping them to observe what is around them.
- Sample question: *What leader do you admire and why?*

Teamwork

- Humans do their best work when working in groups. We need to collaborate and depend on others, showing up for them in return to get big things done well. Talking to your child about friends, school groups and sporting teammates is a good place to start.

- Sample question: *Should teammates be friends?*

Thinking Skills

Creativity

- As machines do increasingly more for us, the human ability to be creative will arguably become our single biggest strength. The pace of innovation is mind-blowing and is only increasing. What is common today did not exist 20 years ago, and your child will thrive if they are hard-wired to be creative with anything they look at.
- Sample question: *What might an alien look like?*

Critical Thinking

- There is so much information and disinformation out there. Today the skill is about searching, interpreting and challenging what we find online. In an age where ready-made answers are so common it is helpful to instil in your child an ability to solve problems themselves, probing and quizzing many solutions until fully satisfied.
- Sample question: *How would you reduce traffic on the roads?*

Philosophy

- Anyone can have a view on anything and you can encourage your child to develop and express theirs. Even seemingly simple questions can help your children explore what is around them which otherwise might not be obvious. This skill is particularly good for tackling 'life's big questions'.

- Sample question: *Should everyone donate money to charity?*

Analytics

- Analytical skills are in high demand. We live in a data-rich world and the ability to process and make sense of it will help your child navigate through it all. Thinking analytically also builds coding skills, which are so important to manage the applications of tomorrow.
- Sample question: *What steps are needed to make a cheese sandwich?*

Feeling Skills

Confidence

- We all want our children to be confident. It can however be a fragile thing which takes time to build up. Conversations around confidence can help children unlock their own inner confidence so that they can always call upon it as needed.
- Sample question: *What is something you learned to do in the past year?*

Empathy

- Mental health is a hot topic. Helping your child to be in touch with their own feelings and with the feelings of those around them has never been more important. You can lay their foundations by frequently discussing feelings and highlighting their role in life.

- Sample question: *Can you name 10 different emotions?*

Resilience

- Resilience can be taught, it is not inherent. Children who display grit, determination and perseverance will push through challenging moments and achieve success. Fostering a growth mindset will help your child always seek out the learning opportunity and thrive.
- Sample question: *Why is it good to fail sometimes?*

Mindfulness

- Being aware of ourselves and how we feel gives us the control needed to let our best selves shine through. Your children can achieve their potential if they can better regulate their thoughts, feelings and actions – and this is something you can discuss with them at a young age.
- Sample question: *What comes first – thoughts or feelings?*

50 fast and fun questions for kids

Here is a handy list of fast and fun questions your kids will love. Dip into them anytime you are in the mood. They come from a longer list of 101 questions for kids, which is a popular article on our website. So if you want more then please visit www.kidcoach.app.

Critical thinking questions

1. *How many grains of sand do you think there are on a typical beach?*
2. *If you could go back in time and change one thing, what would it be and why?*
3. *What would happen if it never rained?*
4. *How could you make £100 by next week if you wanted to?*
5. *Is there life on other planets?*

Debating questions

6. *Should children set their own bedtimes?*
7. *Should everyone donate money to charity?*

8. *Should children have to wear school uniforms?*
9. *Should every child have their own mobile phone?*
10. *Is it right to eat animals?*

Fun communication challenges

11. *How would you describe a tree without saying green, plant or leaves?*
12. *Can you name 10 different emotions?*
13. *Can you say the alphabet backwards?*
14. *Can you talk for one minute about anything without saying "umm" or "err"?*

Alternatives to how was your day

15. *What was the best thing that happened to you today?*
16. *What will you do tomorrow that you did not do today?*
17. *Tell me about something new that you learned today?*
18. *What made you laugh today?*
19. *Who did you play with today?*
20. *What made your teacher smile today?*
21. *What made you really proud today?*
22. *What questions did you ask the teacher today?*
23. *What do you think your teacher/friends/a well-known figure will be doing tonight?*

Getting to know you questions

24. *What are your three greatest strengths?*
25. *What is your favourite subject?*
26. *What makes you different?*
27. *What are your three greatest weaknesses?*

28. *Who do you want to be like when you grow up?*
29. *Who are your best friends and why do you like each other?*
30. *What is the funniest thing you've ever done?*
31. *What motivates you?*

To build resilience

32. *What do you feel grateful for today?*
33. *What is something you can do today that you couldn't last year?*
34. *What do you worry about the most?*
35. *What is a natural talent you have?*
36. *What do you love to learn?*
37. *What makes you happy?*
38. *How important is winning?*
39. *What is your best quality?*
40. *What do you find really easy to do?*
41. *What can you teach others?*

Perfect for the dinner table

42. *If you could just eat one food forever what would it be?*
43. *Where shall we go on holiday next?*
44. *What is one thing you admire about the person on your left?*
45. *If you could swap places with anybody else in the family for one day, who would you pick and why?*
46. *Tell us something about yourself that we probably don't know?*
47. *What is the hardest thing about being a child?*
48. *What three things do we want to do as a family next month?*

49. *If you could choose a new name, what would it be?*

50. *What will we all be doing in 20 years' time?*

APPENDIX III

40 more questions on things kids love

Children engage more easily when talking about something they are passionate about. Here are 40 questions I came up with for a variety of interests. All of them feature in the KidCoachApp along with dozens more topics you can search for.

Animals

1. *Would it be better to be strong like a T-Rex or fast like a Velociraptor?*
2. *If you could create a new animal what would it be like?*
3. *If you discovered a new dinosaur what would you call it?*
4. *What might happen if animals could talk?*
5. *What is the most valuable animal and why?*

Football

6. *Who are the best football managers and why?*
7. *How long do Messi and Ronaldo train for each day?*
8. *What new rules could you invent for the game of football?*
9. *Is it right that footballers get paid millions of pounds?*

10. *Would you rather play exciting football but lose or play boring football and win?*

Harry Potter

11. *Which Hogwarts house would you be sorted into?*
12. *Where do you think Hogwarts School could be?*
13. *How would you explain the game of Quidditch to a Muggle?*
14. *What are seven words to describe Ron Weasley?*
15. *Would you want a real-life Philosopher's Stone?*

Technology

16. *What do you wish you had invented?*
17. *Should you be polite to Alexa when asking for things?*
18. *If you could have a robot arm, would you want one?*
19. *Which is your favourite emoji?*
20. *Are driverless cars a good thing?*

Arts and Crafts

21. *What are five things you can draw with?*
22. *If you invented a new colour, what would you call it?*
23. *If you could create any museum you wanted, what would it be for?*
24. *If you designed a new city what would it be like?*
25. *Where do the best ideas come from?*

Friends

26. *What would you do if your friends wanted to play different games?*
27. *Say your friend couldn't do the monkey bars, what could you say to them?*
28. *Do teammates need to be friends?*
29. *What are 10 different ways to send your friends a party invite?*
30. *How have you and your friends changed each other?*

Games

31. *What are five things that you find fun to do?*
32. *If you invented a new game using playing cards, what would the rules be?*
33. *What do you think is the difference between a sport and a game?*
34. *Can playing video games be a real job?*
35. *How do you play chess?*

School

36. *Should children choose what to learn at school themselves?*
37. *Do you want to be good at maths?*
38. *Is your headteacher a good leader?*
39. *What is your favourite subject?*
40. *What are five school values you remember?*

APPENDIX IV

25 prompting questions to keep conversations going

The secret to a great conversation with kids is what you ask after the first question. There are certain nudging prompts that open up questions wonderfully, and every conversation card I have written in the KidCoachApp has well-worded prompts like this.

Here are 25 of my favourite prompts to get kids talking and thinking:

1. *What might happen next?*
2. *What is this similar to?*
3. *What is this different to?*
4. *What are the pros?*
5. *What are the cons?*
6. *Can you give me an example of what you mean?*
7. *What are the three options you suggest?*
8. *What ideas can we come up with?*
9. *What data or evidence is there to back up what you are saying?*
10. *What can you see/hear/smell taste/touch?*

11. *What is the most important part of all this?*
12. *What three words would you use to describe how you feel about this?*
13. *What would your brother/friend/teacher say about this?*
14. *What percentage of your class would say yes or no?*
15. *How big or small an issue is this?*
16. *What does your gut say?*
17. *Where could you go for more information?*
18. *What's the best question you can ask here?*
19. *How can you get more ideas on this?*
20. *How could you check your answer?*
21. *Whose advice or help could you seek out here?*
22. *What would someone say who disagreed with your view?*
23. *Having thought about this more, do you want to change your mind?*
24. *What would it take for you to change your mind?*
25. *Can you now summarise what you are thinking?*

Nine real-life scripts of conversations with kids

I really love asking kids the sorts of questions I have been writing enthusiastically about in this book, and this is exactly what I do in my podcast Questions To Ask Your Kids. You can listen to it on Apple Podcasts, Spotify, Stitcher or wherever you usually get your podcasts.

At the time of writing, we've published 100+ episodes where I've had the pleasure of speaking to dozens of children of ages 6-12 years old asking them questions from the KidCoachApp. Not only is it fun for them and me, but it gives us a chance to test and tweak our questions live in the app.

Here are some more short snippets from some of the conversations we've had. They might inspire you or give a little illustration of how these types of conversations could go in practice.

Leadership: helping others

Me: I'd like you to think back over the week, what examples have you set for others, Yushan?

Yushan (6 years old): Errmmm I helped my sister go to bed at night time.

Me: Aww that's sweet how old is your sister

Yushan: Errrr... Going into... she's going to be nearly three.

Me: Aww that's nice so you helped put her to bed huh?

Yushan: (Silence)

Me: Yeah that's nice, so are there any other things you want to mention that you are proud of this week that you did to help somebody?

Yushan: I helped the people, err I helped, my errr my mum, dad and sister by making the food.

Me: You helped your mum, dad and sister by making food. Cooking, was that cooking?

Yushan: Yeah

Me: Amazing anything else that comes to mind?

Yushan: Hmm yes. Errr so I helped my friends before I left my school for my school holidays. I helped them by if they fell down I could help them.

Me: If they fell down like in the playground?

Yushan: Yeah in the hard courts.

Me: Aww you literally helped them back up.

Yushan: Yeah.

Leadership: talking about Dumbledore

Me: So Johan, I know you love Harry Potter, do you remember the headmaster of Hogwarts? What do you think makes him such a good headmaster?

Johan (7 years old): He's actually quite kind and he doesn't have much of a temper and he's quite nice and generous. And in number 6 which I do remember, he died for Harry, didn't he.

Me: Yes he did, I hope we haven't spoiled it for anyone hahaha. The first thing you said is he's kind and generous, so do you have to be kind to be a good leader?

Johan: Probably. It makes you a better leader.

Me: Why does it make you a better leader?

Johan: Because if you are not kind, people might not want to do anything really with you... because kind people... if you do something good you will get something back, won't you? And he's kind, that's the good thing he's done and if you are kind, people want to be with you. And that makes them a good leader.

Me: So you have to be kind, and get people to like you. Dumbledore has a lot of power as a headmaster and wizard. Is power important to be a leader?

Johan: Well not actually, you don't need it. Well, you can have power as long as you use it for good.

Critical Thinking: spending £1m on other people

Me: Do you like money? Would you like to be rich one day?

Zahra (8 years old): I don't really like the sound of being rich. Sometimes I do it because I can give money to the poor and to my family but I don't want to be rich because you don't get the adventure of trying to earn money...

Me: ...If you had a million pounds, how would you feel and what would you do?

Zahra: I would give it to people who need it then we could all buy stuff we need. If we all help each other then there will be no arguments or wars left because everyone would have what they want.

Me: What I love about your response is your instinctive reaction to help others. I am not sure everyone would do that so I really appreciate that. So you are saying that you would give away all the 1 million pounds?

Zahra: I already have some money in my piggy bank so I don't need it.

Leadership: using money and power to help people

Me: What would you do if you were mayor of your town for a week?

Mariam (9 years old): Maybe make law and try and stop people from being homeless on the streets...so buy some houses, because I would probably be quite rich as well, so I could buy some houses and put homeless people in them, maybe make a hotel for homeless people.

Me: I love the sentiment that you try to help homeless people...

Mariam: Everything in the shops take it down by £15, if it's more than £15 and if it's under £10 then take it down by half its price.

Me: Wow okay, so a very specific answer about the prices of things and discounts... you mentioned before that you would probably be quite rich, what did you mean by that?

Mariam: Like how the president of the USA has a Whitehouse, if you are a president as well, then you are bound to get money pouring in.

Me: Is that their money that they can use to buy ice cream or pizza or whatever they want or is it the city's money?

Mariam: I think it's the city's money but then it's turning into their money because obviously, they are getting it by working for the city...

Resilience: making mistakes and giving examples

Me: Is it important to make mistakes?

Ansh (10 years old): Erm I guess because then you can never learn from your mistakes, because if you don't learn from your mistakes, then there's nothing to learn from except like schooly things. But if you make a mistake, like lots of people making one certain mistake, they know they won't make it again. But if you have never made a mistake before then there's more of a chance that you will make a mistake, because if you haven't made it before you may be scared to make a mistake

Me: What do you mean by that?

Ansh: It just makes you more anxious and worried all the time. So say dropping a pencil or pen, lots of people have done it so they learn not to keep playing with a pen in their hand. But then if you haven't done that before and you see lots of other people do it, then you will be more anxious and worried that you are going to make a mistake.

Me: Can you think of a mistake you learned from recently?

Ansh: I was going to the toilet and the door was locked and I thought somebody must have locked it from the outside, so I tried to unlock it and it turns out there was actually someone in there and they got really annoyed at me haha.

Creativity: message in a bottle

Me: What message would you leave in a bottle?

Aneri (10 years old): Okay so I would probably write about myself because I want to be known in the future and I would probably write that we think there will be time machines in the future and a lot of progress will be made. I would also write the best flavour of ice cream currently is chocolate brownie flavour ice cream. And I would also write that there are many wars happening and people locked up because of covid so I hope the times are better.

Me: If someone found your message in 100 years what would you want them to think?

Aneri: That the whole world and I were trying to make progress and trying to predict the future and also encourage everybody and for them to also feel that we are humans who are not silly and stupid and we are their ancestors. Like right now people are surprised at how advanced the Indus Valley civilization used to be. I don't want them to think we were dumb and then for them be surprised that we are actually smart.

Me: What is the most important moral to leave behind?

Aneri: That they should not lose hope in anything. And from me, they should be humorous because it is just wrong not to be humorous.

Feelings: talking about holidays and presents

Me: What makes a good present?

Mustafa (11 year old): If you got them a gold chain, a 24-carat gold chain, if they don't care about you then it doesn't make a good present. If you got a homemade jumper, you know, actually spent some love and care I think actually a lot more than material expenses.

Me: How would you feel about getting just one present?

Mustafa:... just because I just got one present it really doesn't matter to me because at least I get one present because at least I am grateful to get at least a present because some people are living on the street in the cold on Christmas instead of in their home.

Me: Will the holidays be just as good if no one got any presents?

Mustafa: Well, I think it's just as good because even though, yes you would get presents normally. If presents weren't a thing, you still get time to catch up with family and loved ones because maybe you are also caught up in each other's lives that you never get to actually see family and people at home that you never get to socialise with.

Critical Thinking: talking about pocket money

Me: How much pocket money should kids get?

Andrea (11 years old): So this depends on the age like my sister is 6 years old and sometimes when she's done something good, my parents will give her a dollar just to reward her. But I feel like as you get older and you start getting chores, like my age I get allowance for making the bed and unpacking the dishwasher, I think it's good that kids get that so they can start saving up. But also if you start giving the kids money you really just don't know what the kids are going to do, it might get lost or they might start to brag about it.

Me: Should parents control what kids spend their money on?

Andrea: So I think you might want to monitor the kid with the money and see what they do with it. So a little bit younger than me, like 7/8 years old. If you go to the toy shop and just kind of leave your kid there for an hour or so and then come back and pick them up I think you would want to tell them to keep the receipt so you can be like "okay why did you buy this, I don't think this is a good purchase", and then if you keep telling them you shouldn't have bought this then they will know what not to waste their money on.

Creativity: designing a restaurant

Me: If you opened a new restaurant what would it be like?

Anita (12 years old): So I would... Make it probably like a buffet with different types of food, something that everyone would enjoy. Because some people go to specific sorts of restaurants, so if you kind of get all of the different types of food in one then a lot of people would go there to just get a bit of everything... Maybe like some from each country, not every single country because that's kind of impossible haha.

Me: What would the inside of this restaurant look like?

Anita: Maybe all little stools all in a row, each with a flag of that country and some food under the flag, that would be quite big. And everything's labelled so it's just like a grab and go get the food. There would be tables all around the outside and in the middle, there would be a circle with all the different foods that you go around getting a bit of anything that you would like.

Me: What would you do to make it the best restaurant it could be?

Anita: I don't know, to make it more accessible there could be like a home delivery kind of thing for more people to get it. Erm because erm that's the main issue with why some people don't want to go to restaurants, because there could be a restaurant that some people really want to go to but it's like two hours away so erm the more accessible it is then the better sales it would be and the more people can enjoy it so maybe it could have loads of different branches.

Notes

Foreword

1. The Little Book Of Thunks:
   https://www.independentthinkingpress.com/books/thelittlebooks/the-little-book-of-thunks/
2. Top 10 work skills for tomorrow:
   https://www.weforum.org/agenda/2020/10/top-10-work-skills-of-tomorrow-how-long-it-takes-to-learn-them/
3. Independent Thinking
   https://www.independentthinking.co.uk/

Introduction

1. The Language of Command blog post
   https://smallsteps.blog/2017/10/22/the-language-of-command/

Chapter One

1. Institute For The Future and Dell Technologies joint report:
   https://www.delltechnologies.com/content/dam/del

ltechnologies/assets/perspectives/2030/pdf/SR1940
_IFTFforDellTechnologies_Human-
Machine_070517_readerhigh-res.pdf

2. Britannica definition of AI:
https://www.britannica.com/technology/artificial-intelligence

3. Cognizant whitepaper on future jobs:
https://www.cognizant.com/whitepapers/21-jobs-of-the-future-a-guide-to-getting-and-staying-employed-over-the-next-10-years-codex3049.pdf

4. OECD on AI:
https://oecdedutoday.com/education-skills-learning-compass-2030/

5. McKinsey report on the future of work:
https://www.mckinsey.com/featured-insights/future-of-work/skill-shift-automation-and-the-future-of-the-workforce

6. McKinsey skills list:
https://www.mckinsey.com/~/media/mckinsey/feat
ured%20insights/future%20of%20organizations/skill
%20shift%20automation%20and%20the%20future%20
of%20the%20workforce/mgi-skill-shift-automation-
and-future-of-the-workforce-may-2018.ashx

7. Pearson resources to help students prepare for the
future: https://www.pearson.com/news-and-research/efficacy/skills-for-today.html

8. Skills Builder umbrella framework of 8 essential skills:
https://www.skillsbuilder.org/

9. Jeff Weiner interview with wired magazine:
https://www.linkedin.com/pulse/jeff-weiner-explains-how-linkedin-diversify-global-nicholas-thompson/

10. Sutton Trust report:
    https://www.suttontrust.com/wp-
    content/uploads/2017/10/Life-Lessons-
    Report_FINAL.pdf
11. Why Schools Kill Creativity, TED Talk by Ken
    Robinson:
    https://www.ted.com/talks/sir_ken_robinson_do_sc
    hools_kill_creativity?language=en
12. OECD Director of Education and Skills quote:
    https://www.oecd.org/education/Envisioning-the-
    future-of-education-and-jobs.pdf
13. Sutton Trust Life Lessons report:
    https://www.suttontrust.com/wp-
    content/uploads/2017/10/Life-Lessons-
    Report_FINAL.pd
14. The Prince's Trust report:
    https://www.princes-trust.org.uk/about-the-
    trust/research-policies-reports/education-report-
    2017?utm_source=twitter_aug&utm_medium=social&
    utm_campaign=education

Chapter Two

1. Talk With Your Kids, Michael E. Parker:
    https://www.goodreads.com/book/show/17433203-
    talk-with-your-kids

2. Interview with Esther Wojciki:
    https://qz.com/1613252/esther-wojcicki-raised-two-
    tech-ceos-and-a-college-professor-whats-her-secret/

3. Nicola Crompton, Happy Home Learning UK, Etsy Shop for learning opportunities on a walk or when eating out: https://www.etsy.com/uk/shop/HappyHomeLearni ng?ref=simple-shop-header-name&listing_id=1061687285

Chapter Three

1. Ariadne Bill at Positive Parenting: https://www.positiveparentingconnection.net/autho r/ariadne/

2. Sue Atkins, Parenting Coach: https://sueatkinsparentingcoach.com/

3. How Conversational Duets Spark Language at Home and in the Community by Hirsh-Pasek & Golinkoff: https://www.tandfonline.com/doi/abs/10.1080/016 3853X.2018.1442114

Chapter Four

1. Dr Lani Watson, University of Oxford, Co-Founder of The Questioning Strengths Method www.theqsm.com
2. News sites for children collated by the Guardian: https://theguardianfoundation.org/programmes/new swise/schools/child-friendly-news
3. Lunch Atop A Skyscraper: https://en.wikipedia.org/wiki/Lunch_atop_a_Skyscr aper

Chapter Five

1. Topsy Page, Talk and Philosophy for Children specialist
   www.topsypage.com

Chapter Six

1. Podcast "Questions To Ask Your Kids" (formerly KidCoach Conversations):
   https://kidcoach.buzzsprout.com/

Chapter Seven

1. The Early Catastrophe by Hart and Risley:
   https://www.aft.org/sites/default/files/periodicals/TheEarlyCatastrophe.pdf

2. NPR critical review of 30 million word gap:
   https://www.npr.org/sections/ed/2018/06/01/615188051/lets-stop-talking-about-the-30-million-word-gap

3. Temple Infant Lab defence of 30 million word gap:
   https://templeinfantlab.com/wp-content/uploads/sites/2/2018/09/GolinkoffHoffRoweTamisLeMondaHirshPasek2018.pdf?fbclid=IwAR2wRypjP2wLVlOrpjhIpu6YawOZcAOVaXBnt2bzO2QyynjObFZeGiJcWqg

4. Education Next balanced review of 30 million word gap:

https://www.educationnext.org/dont-dismiss-30-million-word-gap-quite-fast/

5. A longitudinal investigation of the role of quantity and quality of child-directed speech in vocabulary development by Rowe: https://pubmed.ncbi.nlm.nih.gov/22716950/

6. Beyond the 30-Million-Word Gap: Children's Conversational Exposure Is Associated With Language-Related Brain Function by Romeo et al: https://journals.sagepub.com/doi/full/10.1177/0956 797617742725

7. The Brain Changing Power of Conversation, Harvard Review: https://www.gse.harvard.edu/news/uk/18/02/brain -changing-power- conversation?fbclid=IwAR34p9bX7YKTFU5eatG7geJ JnLPy1zFNSDcoQuQ_UBCUNs1Py81j4ljWVDA

8. Baby Lab study on social distancing and development: https://babylab.brookes.ac.uk/research/social- distancing-and-development

9. Early Maternal Time Investment and Early Child Outcomes, Del Bono et al: https://econpapers.repec.org/article/wlyeconjl/v_3a 126_3ay_3a2016_3ai_3a596_3ap_3af96-f135.htm

10. Philosophy for Children: https://p4c.com/

11. Sapere UK national charity for Philosophy for Children:
https://www.sapere.org.uk/

12. The Philosophical Child by Jana Mohr Lone:
https://www.amazon.co.uk/Philosophical-Child-Jana-Mohr-Lone/dp/1442217332

13. DialogueWorks, trainers of P4C and Thinking Moves:
https://dialogueworks.co.uk/

14. The Education Endowment Foundation evaluation of Philosophy for Children:
https://educationendowmentfoundation.org.uk/projects-and-evaluation/projects/philosophy-for-children

15. The Education Endowment Foundation evaluation of Philosophy for Children effectiveness trial:
https://educationendowmentfoundation.org.uk/projects-and-evaluation/projects/philosophy-for-children-effectiveness-trial

16. The Nuffield Foundation study of non-cognitive impacts of Philosophy for Children:
https://www.nuffieldfoundation.org/project/non-cognitive-impacts-of-philosophy-for-children

17. The Oracy Movement:
https://oracy.inparliament.uk/

18. Voice 21:
https://voice21.org/

19. Oracy Cambridge website:
https://oracycambridge.org/
20. Neil Mercer co-authored paper on conversation to
create academic success:
https://www.ncgs.org/wp-
content/uploads/2017/11/Children%E2%80%99s-
Social-Development-Peer-Interaction-and-Classroom-
Learning.pdf

Chapter Eight

1. A "five whys" example:
https://primeyourpump.com/2019/08/01/the-5-
whys/
2. Definition of "scaffolding":
https://www.edglossary.org/scaffolding/#:~:text=In
%20education%2C%20scaffolding%20refers%20to,ind
ependence%20in%20the%20learning%20process
3. Talking Points by Lyn Dawes
https://www.amazon.co.uk/Talking-Points-
Discussion-Activities-Classroom/dp/0415614597
4. The Perils and Promises of Praise by Carol Dweck
http://mereworth.kent.sch.uk/wp-
content/uploads/2015/04/growth_mindsets_dweck-
praise-effort.pdf

Chapter Nine

1. Atomic Habits by James Clear:
https://jamesclear.com/atomic-habits
2. Anita Cleare, parenting expert and author of The
Work/Parent Switch (UK) / The Working Parent's

Survival Guide (US)
https://anitacleare.co.uk/
3. My wife's coaching business: Emma's Healthy Habits
www.emmashealthyhabits.com

Links

If this book has inspired you to try out the KidCoachApp, I would love you to give it a go.

Featured by the BBC, this handy little app will help you have more meaningful conversations with your kids. It's perfect if you have 6-12 year olds and you are looking for a fast and fun way to get them talking and thinking more!

Please visit the website link below for more question examples, short videos of how different children answer them, numerous thoughtful blog articles, the link to our podcast 'Questions To Ask Your Kids', the bios of our amazing Advisory Board full of education and parenting experts as well as all our social media handles for Instagram, Facebook, LinkedIn and Twitter.

I quit my job to build this lifestyle business, being so passionate about the power of 'Little Big Conversations,' and it's been incredibly rewarding so far. It would be wonderful have you join the thousands of parents already in the 'KidCoach' community.

www.kidcoach.app

Printed in Great Britain
by Amazon

15050223R00119